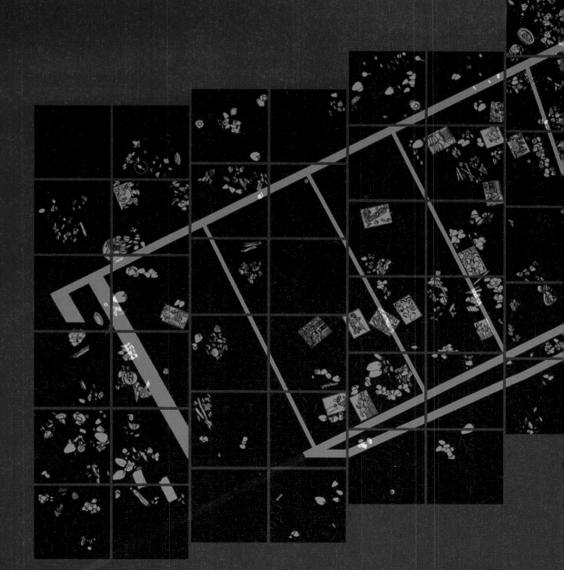

Shinan Shipwreck

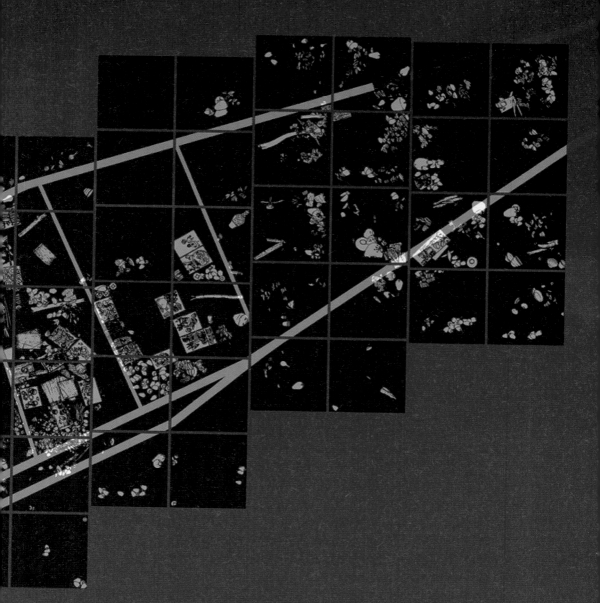

Site Plan of Shinan Shipwreck

# Underwater Archaeology in korea

**UNDERWATER ARCHAEOLOGY IN KOREA**

by the National Research Institute of Maritime Cultural Heritage

Text, Photography © 2016 by the National Research Institute of Maritime Cultural Heritage

Translated in English by Park Haewoon

First published in English by Gongmyoung, #7, 5FLOOR KPIPA, World Cup buk-ro 400, Mapo-gu, Seoul 121-904, Korea. Phone Number 82-2-3153-1378

ISBN 978-89-97870-19-6 93900(CIP2016024497)

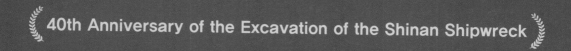

40th Anniversary of the Excavation of the Shinan Shipwreck

# Underwater Archaeology in korea

National Research Institute of
Maritime Cultural Heritage

GONGMYOUNG

# Underwater Archaeology in Korea

Everyone had a dream of exploring treasures ship buried in the sea that described in novels or tales in his/her childhood. Mysteries of the underwater have been unraveled since the early 20th century due to the development of scuba-diving equipments. As a sentence "Continents separate people, the sea brings them together," underwater archaeology, a new academic discipline, began for unraveling mysteries in the sea, the place of connecting the people.

No one expected that underwater archaeology in Korea began with the discovery of a celadon flower vase caught by a fishing net. The Shinan Ship, an international merchant vessel transporting goods along the Maritime Silk Road in the medieval age, resurfaced to us about 650 years later of its last voyage in 1323. The excavations of this shipwreck revealed myriads porcelain vessels and trade goods that clearly show the characteristics of the international maritime trade networks in the fourteenth century. This year marks the 40th anniversary for the discovery of the Shinan Shipwreck.

Mokpo Conservation Center, which was established for conducting conservation of the Shinan Shipwreck, developed into the National Research Institute of Maritime Cultural Heritage that is the only government agency responsible for the Korean underwater cultural heritage. Therefore, the underwater archaeology in Korea has gradually progressed with the discovery of the Shinan Shipwreck as a momentum.

Korean underwater archaeologists have revealed fourteen shipwrecks and more than hundred thousands of artifacts in the West and South Seas in Korea so far. These salvaged hulls and objects clearly exhibit the cultural exchange patterns occurred in sea routes. In summer 2007, immediately after the discovery of a celadon vessel caught with a webfoot octopus off the coast of Daeseom Island in Taean, I arrived at the excavation site at Daeseom Island. When I observed several pieces of salvaged Goryeo celadon vessels, I knew that these objects were produced at kilns in Gangjin. The excavations of the Taean Shipwreck revealed the sunken hull loaded with more than 25,000 Goryeo celadon vessels, and wooden tablets recording the fact: sending celadon vessels fired in kilns in Tamjin Prefecture(present-day Gangjin) to Gaegyeong, the capital of the Goryeo Dynasty. The Taean Shipwreck shipped with high quality celadon vessels were buried under the seabed for over 800 years.

After the excavation of the Taean Shipwreck, the institute excavated shipwrecks off the coast of Mado Island, Yeongheungdo Island in Incheon and Daebudo Island in Ansan. Notably, numerous anchor stones salvaged off the coast of Mado Island and from the Sea of Myeongnyangdaecheop-ro demonstrate that these two places were the key points of the maritime network in Korea during the pre-modern era. On the basis of the achievements of these excavations, the underwater archaeology of Korea could be more highly developed; and the Seohae Research Institute of Maritime Cultural Heritage in Taean will open in 2017.

Thanks to the efforts of few underwater archaeologists, underwater archaeology could have developed into one of the major academic disciplines in Korea in a short period. This book, "Underwater Archaeology in Korea," introduce the results achieved by Korean underwater archaeologists to the public. It is my hope that the readers of this book can feel the true value of the underwater cultural heritage salvaged in Korea.

Lastly, I would like to express my thanks to Korean underwater archaeologists who have achieved notable academic results under the poor researching and investigating conditions.

October 2016

Rha Sunhwa

Administrator of the Cultural Heritage Administration

# Treasure Ships in Korea

Korea is a country surrounded by water on three sides. For many centuries the people of the Korean peninsula have been actively involved in exchange with its neighboring countries and transported domestic goods by exploiting local sea routes. For example, cargo vessels transported grains paid as taxes to Gaegyeong(present-day Gaeseong), the capital of the Goryeo Dynasty, and to Hanyang(present-day Seoul), the capital of the Joseon Dynasty. However, numerous maritime accidents were caused by rapid tidal currents, heavy fogs, and dangerous reefs; and many cargo vessels came to grief in the seas surrounding the Korean peninsula. Although shipwrecks were a source of great misfortune for their crews, the wrecked ships and the many artifacts that sank with them lie preserved under mud, often preserving historical scenes of ancient societies. Therefore, it is reasonable to define the Korean seabed as a living maritime museum that contains vivid evidence of ancient human societies and lifestyles.

The underwater excavation of the Shinan Shipwreck, which was initially conducted in Korea in 1976, was a section of the exhibition. However, at that time there was no particular training for underwater excavation by archaeologists or special underwater survey equipment in Korea, so it fell to divers of the Republic of Korea Navy to carry out underwater investigations. After completing the underwater excavation of the Shinan Shipwreck, the situation remained unchanged for years due to vague fears and real risks associated with the underwater environment.

Since 2002, however, the Research Institute of Maritime Cultural Heritage has secured the budget required for further academic underwater excavations, including much-needed funds for equipment, and has trained underwater archaeologists. By building up our field experiences very gradually, the institute has succeeded in pioneering underwater excavation in Korea, and produced remarkable achievements that have shed light on the life of Korean people in the past.

Our underwater excavations have brought to light many historical facts and events that are not recorded in historical sources. The celadon prunus vase was called *jun*(樽) in the Goryeo Period, and was used as a storage vessel for precious foodstuffs such as honey and sesame oil, as well as liquors. In addition, it was found that the ship was transporting antlers of a deer species already extinct in Korea to Gaegyeong in the Goryeo Period.

At present, Korean underwater archaeology, which thankfully has moved beyond the stage of conducting underwater surveys with the assistance of the Republic of Korea Navy, is leading Asia and the world by pioneering its way to the highest level. Korea is one of the few countries to possess underwater exploration ships. A prominent Japanese underwater archaeologist confessed that Japanese underwater archaeology is now at a lower level than Korean underwater archaeology. Even underwater archaeologists of the MEDCs have learned from the investigation methods and experiences of Korea's underwater archaeologists.

In these circumstances, the staff of the institute and Korean underwater archaeologists asked themselves what they could do beyond the publication of excavation reports and the exhibition of excavation results. We, at the Institute, felt that, as the year 2016 marks the fortieth anniversary of the beginning of Korean underwater archaeology with the excavation of the Shinan Shipwreck, it would be appropriate to publish a book commemorating this auspicious anniversary and to introduce the proud achievements of Korean underwater archaeology to the general public.

Certainly, we did not simply dive into the sea with the dream of publishing book on Korean underwater archaeology. As the results of our efforts continued to accumulate, our dream grew bolder. In order to encourage ourselves not to be lazy, we wrote about our efforts to salvage one of many fragments of history lying buried under the seabed.

It is our hope that this book will provide readers with an interesting introduction to an eye-opening encounter with treasure ships and underwater archaeology in Korea.

On behalf of all the authors

October 2016

Moon Whansuk

Contents

## Part 1
...........
# History of the Korean Underwater Archaeology

## Part 2
..........

# Time Capsules in the Sea, the Search for Lost History

Part **1**

# History of the Korean
## Underwater Archaeology

# Treasure Ships and the Beginnings of the Underwater Archaeology

Chapter 1

# Treasure Ships and the Beginnings of the Underwater Archaeology

There have been many exciting adventure and action films in which the heroes and heroines discover the remains of an ancient civilization or embark upon a quest to find hidden treasures. Certainly, these movies often portray stereotypical archaeologists wearing a felt and unraveling the mysteries of ancient peoples as they carefully brushing soil and debris off artifacts.

As such, archaeology, which pushes the bounds of adventure and exploration, is an academic field that reconstructs past cultures by investigating the material remains of ancient peoples and studies cultural changes in ancient societies and how they came about. Underwater archaeology, in other words, the study of archaeological materials lying in seas, rivers and lakes, is a sub-discipline of archaeology.

Fundamentally, underwater archaeology uses the same research methods as archaeological surveys conducted at ground level. Nevertheless, the material types and remaining patterns of artifacts and features salvaged from underwater sites differ markedly from those unearthed from land-based sites, since they are located under a particular environment, water.

Scholars are now able to uncover information related to the maritime activities of diverse cultures ranging from the prehistoric era to modern times. While artifacts that have buried under the ground are continuously destroyed or simply perish, sunken hulls and other artifacts lying covered with mud and silt beneath the sea keep and conserve their original shape for a much longer period of time than those covered with soil.

In particular, hulls and artifacts that sank beneath the sea at a particular time and place are time capsules that contain valuable information on the living conditions and social aspects of past societies. Therefore, material remains uncovered from the sea constitute an invaluable source of information that cannot be found in artifacts and features discovered on land.

Sunken hulls have yielded an abundance of organic matter that can only be preserved at land-based sites under particular conditions, such as wetland sites. For instance, Mado Shipwreck No. 3 contained wooden combs that were well so preserved

Discovery of Batches of Celadon Lidded Cups in Mado Shipwreck No. 2

**Organic Artifacts Rarely Found at Land-based Sites**

1 Wooden comb recovered from Mado Shipwreck No. 3

2 Fish bones recovered from Mado Shipwreck No. 3

3 Bamboo hat recovered from Dalido Shipwreck

4 Persimmons dried in the Goryeo Period recovered from Daebudo Shipwreck No. 2

that it could even be used today. Furthermore, it seems that fish bones retrieved from Mado Shipwreck No. 3 are the remains of dried fish. As with dried pollack, yellowish fish fillets were found between the bones as if they had been buried just a few months ago. Moreover, dried persimmons taken from Daebudo Shipwreck No. 2 introduced underwater archaeologists to the delightful concept of "time slip." As the red flesh of the persimmons had been preserved, the investigators were able to experience the miracle of smelling persimmons that had been dried in the Goryeo Period. This ability to investigate preserved organic matter is one of the most attractive features of underwater archaeology.

The systematic excavation of underwater sites was begun in the mid-twentieth century. Prior to that, underwater investigations were conducted by divers who were not trained in archaeological survey methods. Underwater archaeology is a young academic discipline that is associated with the development of maritime surveying equipment from the nineteenth to the early twentieth century. In Korea, underwater archaeology was only introduced in the 1970s. Therefore, it is an academic discipline with excellent growth potential.

## Types of Underwater Sites

Which types of sites remain underwater in seas and rivers? Shipwrecks are the representative structures found in the course

The Anjwa Shipwreck

of underwater excavations. Ships that were sunk by sudden gusts of wind, strong tidal waves, heavy fog, collisions with rocks, strong typhoons or sailors' mistakes were doomed to become shipwrecks.

Shipwrecks are significant materials for studying the shipbuilding techniques and nautical skills of earlier societies. Moreover, the majority of wrecked ships were either international trading vessels or cargo vessels transporting grains paid in tax and tax-in-kind. Therefore, the cargos contained in shipwrecks are invaluable evidence for studying the cultural and social features of long vanished societies. Although the hull was never found, thousands of Goryeo celadon porcelains were excavated from a wreck off the

coast of Yamido Island, providing important information about Goryeo society.

Investigation of Brick Building at Port Royal, Jamaica

In addition to shipwrecks, ports, shipyards, sea defenses and floating houses are all classified as underwater sites. For example, the sea defense facility in Cheonghaejin that was established by Jang Bogo in the Unified Silla Period(828 AD) is also regarded as an underwater site. The remaining features of such sites might be located both below water and on land or above water. After such sites fell into disuse or were destroyed, only the features below water survived.

In addition, historic sites have been submerged by the construction of dams or by natural disasters such as earthquakes or tsunamis, while some Paleolithic and Neolithic sites have been submerged due to the rising sea level. Although there have been no excavations of such sites in Korea, many uninvestigated archaeological sites are located in submerged areas. Port Royal in southeastern Jamaica is one of the world's most famous underwater sites. On 7 June 1692, about 2,000 buildings and 5,000 houses were destroyed by a series of three earthquakes, which were accompanied by tsunamis. In 1895, divers of Great Britain's Royal Navy discovered the remains of the town; and a site distribution map was produced in the twentieth century based on the findings ultrasonic surveys.

## Treasure Hunting vs. Archaeological Excavation

In the eyes of the public, seeking 'lost treasures' in deep seas may be nothing more than a fairy tale. Nevertheless, it is a dream and an adventure for certain people who stake their whole life on it. Mel Fisher, an American treasure hunter, spent sixteen years of his life exploring the waters off coast of the Gulf of Mexico in an attempt to find a Spanish ship that sank in 1622. Finally, in 1985, he discovered the Nuestra Senora de Atocha. He spent about fifteen million US dollars on searching and salvaging the wreck, but the value of the treasures she yielded amounted to no less than four hundred million dollars.

Underwater excavation began when people tried their luck at finding treasures in the sea. Before the mid-twentieth century, treasure hunters who were uneducated in the field of archaeological surveys dived into the sea in search of gold and silver objects and precious antiques.

In Korea, there were several attempts to fund such buried treasures. Treasure hunters searched for ships that had been sent to the bottom in the Sino-Japanese War, the Russo-Japanese War, and the Second World War in the waters off Uldo Island in Incheon, Ulleungdo Island, Geojedo Island, Jukdo Island in Jindo, and the sea of Gunsan. They conducted their explorations on the basis of inaccurate rumors that the ships contained gold and silver bars, the sinews of war; but there have been no cases of discovery of such valuable treasures. Rather, these resulted in criminal cases such as stock manipulation scandals and fraud cases.

Moreover, even when they did succeed in finding treasure, there was no great jackpot for the treasure hunters. Many of the artifacts salvaged from the sea, such as Goryeo celadon and white porcelain vessels, are cultural heritages, needless to say. In Korea, the government even transfers the ownership of objects related to important historical events in modern times to the national museum. For example, the objects contained in the Goseungho, a ship that was sunk in the Sino-Japanese War and eventually located off the coast of Uldo Island, Incheon, were vested in the government.

The Goseungho was a British merchant ship borrowed by the Chinese government to transport Chinese troops to Korea during the Sino-Japanese War. The ship was sunk by the Japanese Navy in

1894. Due to rumors that it had contained five tons of horseshoe-shaped silver ingots and Mexican silver coins, excavations of the ship were conducted in 1925, 1935, 1979 and 2001 by treasure hunters. The artifacts shown in the photos were salvaged in 2001. In fact, the Goseungho was the first treasure ship ever salvaged in Korea; but, despite the rumors, the ship contained few silver objects.

Therefore, any search for the treasure ship was a reckless challenge doomed to failure for the treasure hunters who spent years of their life in Korea. Moreover, treasure hunters are generally obsessed with finding priceless objects including precious metal items and antiques; as such, they are not concerned about artifacts and archaeological features, which they consider valueless, and often damage or destroy them in their frantic search for treasure. In addition, they do not produce photos or illustrations of the excavation site, since possessing precious artifacts is their only purpose. Therefore, it is often impossible to determine the context of the salvaged objects in any detail, including the ship that contained them, their location, and the underwater environment in which they were found. Therefore, objects salvaged by treasure hunters generally lose their academic value due to the loss of historical and academic information. And, given that even a systemically conducted archaeological excavation can also be defined as a kind of act of destruction, treasure hunting is a definite act of heritage destruction.

Illegal robbery is a far more serious problem than treasure hunting, as well as being a serious crime. Moreover, the site has been seriously damaged by looting. Looters only regard the value of a cultural heritage in monetary terms, and thus do not treat artifacts and shipwrecks with no monetary value carefully. Rather, looters often consider them to be obstacles to their goal and seriously destroy a site while randomly collecting artifacts. Moreover, artifacts are damaged by the thoughtless treatments of looters.

Ironically, several underwater sites were brought to light with the arrest of looters. The Myeongnyangdaecheop-ro(Ave.) sea is a representative case in this respect. Underwater excavations conducted at the site since 2012 have revealed Goryeo celadon

**10** | 2011년 11월 18일 금요일    사회

# 40억대 고려향로 등 무더기 도굴

### 난파선 찾아다니며 문화재 70여점 빼돌려…염산으로 이물질 제거 일부는 크게 훼손

서울지방경찰청 광역수사대 관계자가 18일 도굴꾼으로부터 압수한 고려 중기 문화재 '청자양각연지수금문방형향로'를 들어보이고 있다.    이상섭 기자/babtong@

Arrest of Looters of Precious Heritage Objects including Goryeo Celadon Valued at Four Billion Won
Newspaper article dated November 2011

Treasure Ships and the Beginnings of the Underwater Archaeology **29**

porcelains and Joseon cannons. Of these finds, there has been considerable debate about the *sososeungjachongtong*(少少勝字銃筒), a cannon known to have been manufactured by Yun Deokyeong in 1588, before the outbreak of the *Imjin Waeran*(The Japanese Invasion of Korea, 1592-98), because it is thought to have been used in the Battle of Myeongnyang.

However, the underwater excavations conducted after the arrest of looters have some limitations with regard to achieving academic development. In order to prevent damage to underwater sites and artifacts and to obtain more valuable academic results, it is essential that underwater investigations be undertaken by specialists who are educated in the field of underwater surveys and archaeology.

# Time Capsules of History: Excavation of the Underwater Cultural Heritage

# Time Capsules of History: Excavation of the Underwater Cultural Heritage

During the 2010 FIFA World Cup hosted in South Africa, an unexpected superstar emerged to gain even greater popularity than the football players, namely, Paul the Octopus, an "animal oracle." Paul predicted the winners of each of the seven matches that the German team played, as well as the winner of the final, Spain. The Spanish Government granted honorary citizenship to Paul.

Before Paul won a worldwide reputation as a fortune-teller, a webfoot octopus left an indelible mark on the history of Korean underwater archaeology, as it found an artifact in the water. Webfoot octopuses are known to block the aperture of a conch

A Webfoot Octopus Caught with a Celadon Bowl in Taean

with small shells or stones after laying their eggs inside it. This webfoot octopus, which blocked an aperture using a celadon dish, was caught by a fisherman along with the dish. This ultimately provided the momentum to discover the Taean Shipwreck and to begin underwater excavations of the sea in Taean, a rich repository of Korean underwater artifacts sometimes referred to as "Taean, the Gyeongju of the Sea."

## Beginning of the Underwater Excavation

A total of fourteen shipwrecks including the Shinan Ship have been excavated from the seabed and mudflats in Korea, as well as five buried sites densely packed with artifacts. Except for two underwater sites at Jindo Island and Yamido Island in Gunsan, which were identified from the statements of looters, underwater investigations of all the other sites were undertaken to confirm the statements of fishermen and scuba divers who frequently reported their accidental discoveries of artifacts to their local government offices.

People have frequently reported the discovery of cultural remains on the mainland. Considering the relative ease of identifying such archaeological sites, reports of them are less important than reports of sites in the marine environment. Myriad cultural relics remain in Korea, so many in fact that the whole country is referred to as a "museum," as people have resided in the Korean Peninsula since the prehistoric era. Therefore, people who have some knowledge of our cultural heritage are easily able to find archaeological sites and artifacts.

By contrast, even though there have been many shipwrecks off the coast of Korea, it is difficult to locate them because they are covered by a deep blue shroud of seawater. Moreover, in most cases, the remains of their hull structures are scattered in all directions, and are usually washed away by strong offshore currents and waves. Despite such difficulties, underwater sites have often been accidentally located by the nets of fishermen rather than by specialists. Therefore, the excavation of significant underwater sites in Korea is undertaken according to the reports of fishermen. A fisherman who found a celadon object in Taean is a representative case of this phenomenon. For these reasons, fishermen and scuba divers who report the artifacts they retrieve to the government office are the hidden pillars of and best contributors to the excavation of our underwater cultural heritage.

## The Exploration of Underwater Sites

Underwater surveys are generally undertaken following reports of the discovery of artifacts. The preliminary survey aims to detect shipwrecks or buried sites that are rich in artifacts. Aquanautics is the most infallible method of identifying or confirming the existence of an underwater site, although it is also the most time-consuming method.

The excavation of the Yeongheungdo Shipwreck, which was salvaged in 2013, was begun in 2012 with a survey of the artifact-scattered area lying 300 meters east-west and 500 meters north-south. This investigation team divided the area into a grid composed of fifty-meter-square sections, and slowly conducted the preliminary survey from the northeast sector. If this area were located on the ground, the preliminary survey would have been completed within five days. However, the detailed preliminary survey of the site took about sixty days(from the end of April to August) to find the shipwreck. Therefore, it took two days to survey each section of the grid.

Still, this site was a good place to conduct an underwater survey compared to other seas as visibility in the seawater is relatively good, and the seabed is deposited with sand and pebbles; in fact,

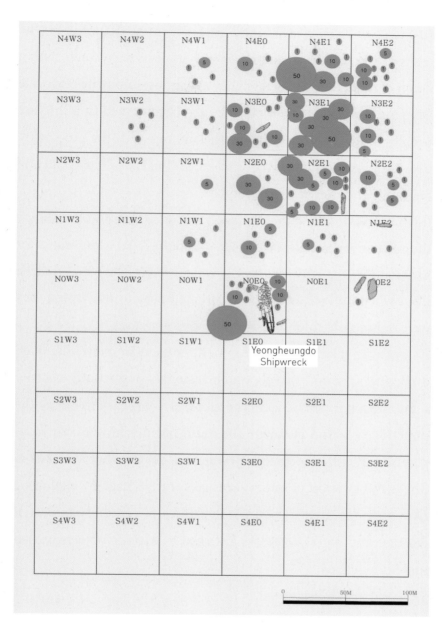

| N4W3 | N4W2 | N4W1 | N4E0 | N4E1 | N4E2 |
| N3W3 | N3W2 | N3W1 | N3E0 | N3E1 | N3E2 |
| N2W3 | N2W2 | N2W1 | N2E0 | N2E1 | N2E2 |
| N1W3 | N1W2 | N1W1 | N1E0 | N1E1 | N1E2 |
| N0W3 | N0W2 | N0W1 | N0E0 | N0E1 | N0E2 |
| S1W3 | S1W2 | S1W1 | S1E0 | S1E1 | S1E2 |
| S2W3 | S2W2 | S2W1 | S2E0 | S2E1 | S2E2 |
| S3W3 | S3W2 | S3W1 | S3E0 | S3E1 | S3E2 |
| S4W3 | S4W2 | S4W1 | S4E0 | S4E1 | S4E2 |

Yeongheungdo
Shipwreck

0    50M    100M

**Grids of the Underwater Survey Area at the Yeongheungdo Shipwreck Site**
The green circles in the illustration mark the location of porcelains and their quantities.

if the ship had been located at the southern end of the investigated area, the investigation period would have lasted for more than 120 days.

In cases where shipwrecks and artifacts are not exposed on the seabed or buried in a mudflat, or are sunk in deep water with a depth of more than 30 meters, they are almost impossible to locate using only aquanautics. Moreover, goods contained in a ship are usually widely dispersed during the sinking; thus the probability of finding artifacts in the reported area is less than 10 percent, and few hull structures are ever found.

It is also worth noting that the West Sea(Yellow Sea) of Korea, unlike the Mediterranean Sea or the seas of South Asia, is notorious for its low visibility, which generally ranges from just 1 to 2 meters. Even when hull structures were situated near to the divers, they were only able to find them by touch in some cases.

As such, special survey equipment is used to overcome such difficulties. Sound travels much faster through water(1,500 m/s) than through air(340 m/s). Therefore, it is not easy to detect the direction of sound in water. The multi-beam echo sounder, side-scan sonar, and sub-bottom profiler are devices that are used to detect the location of underwater cultural heritage by exploiting the characteristics of sound. In addition, remotely-operated vehicles and metal detectors are used to explore objects buried under the seabed.

# ● Equipment Used in the Exploration of Underwater Sites ●

## Side-scan Sonar

The side-scan sonar is a device used to detect sunken hulls and artifacts among other things. In order to get closer to the bottom of deep seawater, side-scan transducers are placed in a "tow fish" and pulled along by a tow cable. This equipment, which may be towed by a surface vessel, produces images of the seafloor by emitting conical pulses across a wide angle perpendicular to the path of the sensor through the water; and receives reflections from the seafloor from this fan-shaped . The intensity and shadow of the acquired data are directly related with the back-scattering and roughness factors of the materials on the seabed. In cases where the seafloor is deposited with silt and mud, the received acoustics are very weak as they reflect most of the pulses. However, the equipment receives strong acoustics from a seafloor that has strong roughness factors or rocks due to the high back-scattering factors. Since the same material has identical back-scattering factors, materials on the seafloor can be identified by analyzing the different back-scattering factors.

Side-scan Sonar

**Image Produced by Side-scan Sonar**
The center of the image is marked in black because a side-scan sonar emits fan-shaped pulses down toward the seafloor. A porcelain object is clearly marked in the image.

## Remotely-Operated Vehicle

A remotely-operated vehicle operated by the crew of a vessel is a very useful piece of equipment for exploring artifacts and sunken hulls buried in the subfloor of a dangerous body of sea. It is equipped with cameras that transmit video footage in real-time, ultrasonic devices, and a scan sonar, and can salvage artifacts using its robotic arms. As with the exploration of the Titanic, it has been used as the most advantageous device for investigating underwater sites in the West Sea, which is characterized by strong tidal currents, low visibility, and a seafloor deposited with soft mud. The *Crabster*, a remotely-operated vehicle developed by the Korea Research Institute of Ships and Ocean Engineering, was built to investigate underwater sites located in extreme marine conditions such as the West Sea in Korea. Unlike other remotely-operated vehicles that are driven by a propeller, the *Crabster* has legs that enable it to move on the seafloor like a crayfish; thus it does not obstruct the view formed by mud. It is also equipped with a scanning sonar with 360° rotation, a precision supersonic camera, a USBL(ultra-short base line) system, and a flow meter.

The *Crabster*, a remotely-operated vehicle developed to conduct surveys in the West Sea of Korea, was tested in the underwater excavation site off Mado Island in Taean. The test proved that the *Crabster* is very reliable and performs well in underwater excavations as it was able to accurately detect and salvage various artifacts, such as iron caldrons, from the seafloor.

## Multi-beam Echo Sounder

The multi-beam echo sounder is a survey device used in underwater investigation to determine a sub-marine topography. It produces three-dimensional images in real time by emitting 256 sound waves on the seabed and then receiving the returning sound waves. The device vertically emits and receives sound waves, and calculates the return time, when surveying the submarine topography. The photo on the right shows a multi-beam echo sounder image of the Nanjido Sea in Seosan. An artificial fish shelter is visible in the image.

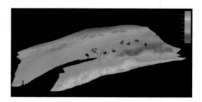

**Image Produced by a Multi-beam Eco Sounder**
The water becomes deeper as the color changes from red to blue.

## Sub-bottom profiler

This piece of equipment is used to locate alien features including shipwrecks and artifacts buried in layers of sediment under the seafloor. It projects sound waves into the sediment, and produces cross-sectional diagrams by recording the signals that are continuously reflected from the sediment. This diagram indicates the sub-bottom structure, the remains of the hull, and the artifacts. The figure on the left clearly shows that different sound waves are detected in the spot where Mado Shipwreck No. 3(red circle) is buried. As shown in the figure on the right, this equipment produces three-dimensional images of the features. One notable fact is that signals(black circle) from a feature were detected 15 meters north of Mado Shipwreck No. 3, raising the possibility that another shipwreck is buried in this spot.

Parametric Quattro SBP Images of the Mado Shipwreck No. 3 Site

## Metal Detector

A metal detector is a device that detects the presence of metal objects in the vicinity of the user. Metal detectors are useful for finding metal inclusions hidden within objects, or metal objects buried underground, such as iron caldrons. Moreover, they can detect bronze objects that have no magnetic force. In general, investigators use a portable metal detector, but tow-type detectors, such as the side-scan sonar, have been used recently.

**Metal Detector**
A metal detector is used to locate objects buried under the floor of a shallow sea.

## Discovery of the Sunken Hull

When investigators identify features detected by equipment or discovered by divers, they should remain calm. The first thing to do is to discern whether it sank in the modern period or in the ancient period. In general, most features found by underwater survey systems are not hulls that sank in the remote past, but rather ocean and marine waste such as plastic ropes. Nevertheless, investigators do find the hulls of ships that sank in the ancient and medieval periods by tracing the signs left by them persistently.

**A Modern Wooden Ship that Sank in the Waters off Yeosu, Jeollanam-do Province**
Side-scan sonar images made it possible to detect a feature presumed to be a sunken ship(Left). Divers identified it as a modern wooden vessel(Right).

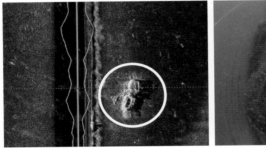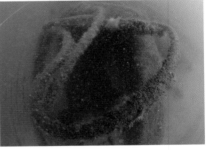

For example, it can be detected some signs at the site of an ancient shipwreck. Cargos were scattered around the hull; and in some cases, large wooden materials, parts of the hull, are scattered. Investigators surmised that Mado Shipwreck No. 1, which was identified in 2009, was an ancient shipwreck, since large wooden materials and a large cargo of celadon bowls and other goods was distributed across the seafloor. Of the Goryeo shipwrecks excavated to date, Mado Shipwreck No. 3 was the one in the most intact condition. When it was first identified, wooden materials were exposed on the seafloor; and three antlers(cargos) were found.

Batches of
Celadon Vessels
on the Seafloor.
Goods Shipped on
Mado Shipwreck
No. 1(Left),
Parts of the
Wooden Hull
Exposed during
the Excavation of
Mado Shipwreck
No. 3(Right)

## Preparations for the Excavation of a Shipwreck

After identifying the size and orientation of the hull, investigators divide the excavated area into sections to create a grid. Although the dimensions of each grid depend on the condition of the site, usually a grid is 1 meter long and 1 meter wide. Investigators install grids made of iron or rope in the excavated area. When rope grids are installed, investigators can easily remove silt covering the excavated area because of the flexibility of the ropes. However, these are moved easily by tidal currents and contact with the investigators. However, these are moved easily by tidal currents and contact with the investigators. During the underwater excavations, therefore, iron grids are main frames; and ropes are used for installing

Installation of Iron
Grids(Left) and
Rope Grids(Right)
at the Taean
Shipwreck Site

subsidiary grids.

The main purpose of installing a grid is to collect as much information as possible, as well as salvaging artifacts and structures. In order words, not only an artifact itself but also the spatial location of an artifact is a significant piece of archaeological information. The installation of grid is the most effective method of collecting such information. This is similar to an excavation of a land-based site. Nevertheless, the installation of a grid is more essential in an underwater excavation due to seawater's low visibility.

## Removal of Mud from Sunken Hulls and Artifacts

In excavations conducted on the ground, investigators generally remove soil using shovels and trowels. However, sucking out water containing silt is the most efficient method of removing silt during an underwater excavation. There are two types of equipment for removing silt during an underwater excavation, namely, air lifts and vacuum pumps.

An air lift is a type of pump that injects compressed air into the bottom of the discharge pipe, which is immersed in liquid. The compressed air mixes with the liquid to form an air-water mixture less dense than the rest of the liquid around it, which is therefore displaced upwards through the discharge pipe by the surrounding liquid of a higher density. Operators carefully control the air valve to maintain the proper level of buoyancy, since it will become

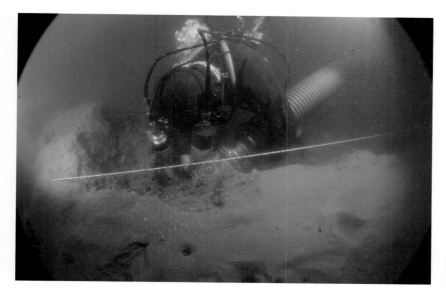

excessively buoyant in an instant if operated incorrectly. When an air lift pump is afloat, the operator can adjust its buoyancy by attaching lead weights to the air injector.

Recently, this device has not been used at underwater excavation sites because its strong suction power hampers detailed excavation work and damages artifacts. The underwater excavation team used this device from the excavation of the Shinan Shipwreck(1976) until the excavation of the Taean Shipwreck(2008).

Recently, a Korean underwater excavation team used a vacuum pump to remove silt. Its operating principle is similar to that of a vacuum cleaner. The amount of silt that this device can suck depends on the diameter of the discharge pipe. A large pipe(15 centimeters in diameter) is used in preliminary excavations, while a small pipe(7-8 centimeters in diameter) is used when excavating sunken hulls containing artifacts. It is an appropriate device for revealing small objects due to its constant suction power. Small hidden objects contained in mud, such as coins, can be filtered out by passing the mud through wire netting on the deck of the exploration ship.

## Actual Measurement and Photography in Underwater Excavation

During an underwater excavation, investigators are able to collect archaeological information by recording all manner of data, including the types of salvaged artifacts and features, and their locations, producing actual measurements of the hulls and artifacts, and taking photos or videos of the underwater conditions.

In particular, the production of actual measurements is one of the most important tasks of an underwater excavation survey. At a land-based site, the entire plan of dwellings or other buildings can be produced in the form of photos or stereoscopic images. However, an actual measurement survey of the entire structure of

The Investigators Who Took the Actual Measurements (Left) and Photo of Mado Shipwreck No. 2(Right)

a hull and the distribution pattern of artifacts is the only method capable of showing and recording the entire plan of an underwater site. When underwater, investigators can only take shots of limited parts of a site due to the low visibility; and even then they can only use a wide-angle lens with a high distortion rate.

Perhaps surprisingly, the actual measurement method used at an underwater site is almost identical to that used at a land-based site. One notable difference in an underwater excavation is that the investigators produce a plan on squared tracing film, which is highly water-resistant, and has bursting strength, rather than on squared paper. Other than this, investigators draw the plan of the site using a pencil, an eraser and a tape measure, as with excavations on terra firma.

After producing horizontal plans, investigators conduct level

Illustration of Mado Shipwreck No. 2

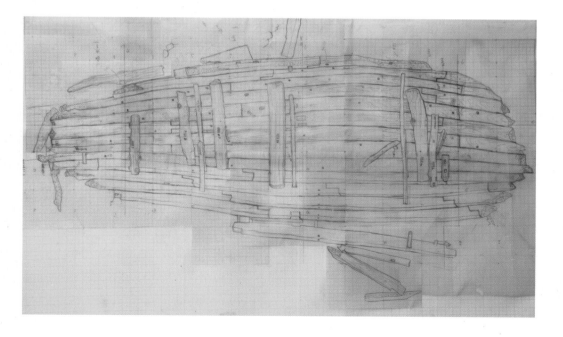

surveys of the site after setting the base point, and then produce sectional plans of the site. In this way, the entire plan of a hull, which is hard to see underwater, can be easily identified in an illustration.

As with excavations on the ground, all the processes of an underwater investigation, including preparatory works, installation of the grid, taking photos of the artifacts, and post-works are recorded in the form of photographs and videos. In order to take photos underwater, water-proofing equipment is essential. Moreover, the risks faced by investigators due to strong water pressure, tidal currents and poor visibility, and the security of the site for taking photos, have to be considered. After considering these factors, the investigators should secure the site in accordance with the direction of the tidal currents, and resolve such problems as diffused reflections.

## Salvaging Hulls and Artifacts

After collecting the artifacts and structures exposed by removing mud and silt from the seafloor, they are raised from the water. This process is called "salvation." Damage prevention is the most important aspect of this process. The basic method consists in placing the artifacts into containers or wrapping them with buttresses for floating. In addition, various methods can be applied to salvage artifacts and hulls in accordance with their sizes and shapes.

1 Putting a wooden tablet in the container
2 Recovering the Skeletal Remains of a Duck
3 Salvaging Rice Seeds
4 Salvaging Batches of Celadon Bowls

For example, some items—including wooden tablets, bamboo slips, long-thin wooden objects, and ropes—require careful handling during the salvation process. In particular, investigators should try to avoid touching wooden tablets and bamboo slips to as not to erase any letters that may be inscribed on their surface. Investigators are able to collect them effectively by using plastic containers or pipes. Small objects and organic matters including grains, straws and fish bones can be easily salvaged by placing them in bottles with a cap, plastic containers, and ziploc bags. However, investigators must be careful not to lose or destroy small objects during the process of storing them in packing containers. Porcelain vessels, which account for the majority of the artifacts

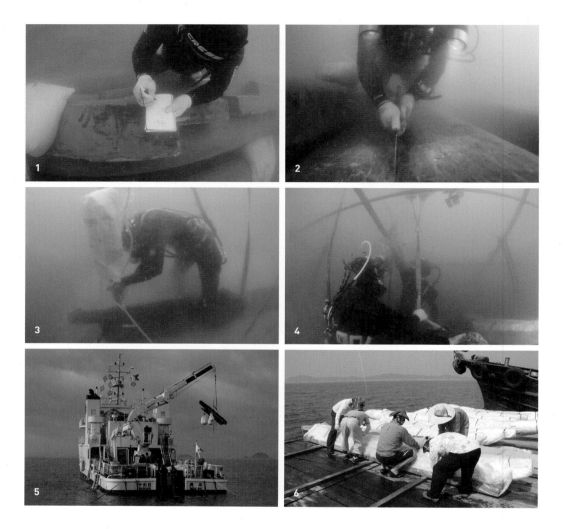

**Procedure for Salvaging the Hull**

1 Identifying the hull's structure
2 Disassembling the hull
3 Fixing the hull on a support
4 Lifting the hull using air bags
5 Salvaging the hull using a crane
6 Wrapping

salvaged in the underwater excavations, are often found in the packed condition in which they were shipped, or are found spread across a wide area due toed by tidal currents. In the former case, batches of porcelain should be put into plastic containers in the order of their registration number to avoid losing valuable information. After lifting artifacts and hulls on deck, investigators produce photos and record them. After completing these procedures, the artifacts will be securely packed.

Of the fourteen shipwrecks excavated in Korea, the hulls of twelve ships were salvaged after disassembling them into several parts. Mado Shipwreck Nos. 3 and 4 have not yet been salvaged. The disassembly method has some advantages in that it can be used to salvage a wreck at low coast, and facilitates the transportation and conservation of such artifacts. The procedure is as follows:

1. The jointing method and structure of the hull are examined.
2. The wooden tenon joints(*Jangsak* and *Pisak*) are disassembled and sawed by broadening the gap between the planks.
3. The dismantled parts of the hull are placed on a support and fixed with wide elastic bands.
4. The parts are elevated using air pockets.
5. The floated structures are lifted onto the deck of the exploration ship by a crane.
6. After supplying the salvaged structures with sufficient moisture, they are packed and wrapped with felt and vinyl.

Regarding the Vasa, a Swedish shipwreck, and Nanhai No. 1 in China, in both cases the investigation team concerned salvaged the entire hull, which lay buried under the seafloor, without any dismantling, after considering the condition and significance of the hull and the artifacts contained in it. Full-scale excavation and conservation treatments were or are now being conducted in the respective labs. Although this is an expensive and time-consuming method, it has some advantages in that investigators are able to conduct a more detailed investigation; and damage to the hull can be minimized.

# Chapter 3

## Tales of the Shinan Ship, the First Found Shipwreck in Korea and the Largest Treasure Ship in the World

Chapter 3

# Tales of the Shinan Ship, the First Found Shipwreck in Korea and the Largest Treasure Ship in the World

If we take a ferry at Mokpo that travels due northwest for over three hours, we will arrive at Jeungdo Island, a fairly large island located at the northernmost point of Shinan-gun County. The island's original Korean name is *Siruseom*(Steamer Island) because it is characterized by well-drained soil layers, like a steamer. However, people usually call it *Bomulseom*, meaning "Treasure Island," rather than by its original name because the Shinan Shipwreck, the largest treasure ship in the world, was excavated off the coast of this island.

In 1975, a fisherman named Choi Hyeonggeun hauled in his fishing net only to find that it contained six porcelain vessels, including a celadon vase, off the coast of Bangchuk-ri, Jeungdo-myeon, Shinan. However, Mr. Choi left these objects lying neglected under the floor of his house because he did not realize their true value. The following year, his younger brother reported the vessels to Shinan-gun County Office; but the local officials did not believe that such valuable goods could have been found in the sea, failed to identify the objects as artifacts, and considered him to be nothing more than a swindler seeking compensation. The porcelain vessels were only revealed as priceless celadon wares produced in the Song and Yuan Dynasties in China after their discovery was reported to the Cultural Properties Administration. According to local residents, many high-quality porcelains had previously been caught in fishing nets in the waters around the island, but they tended to use them either as chamber pots or bowls for dog food, or sold them off to junk dealers.

Shortly thereafter, some more Chinese porcelain vessels were caught in another fisherman's net. As rumors of a sunken treasure ship lying off the coast of Jeungdo Island began to spread, looters flocked to the area. The police arrested robbers who were in possession of numerous expensive, high-quality porcelain vessels in September 1976, after which the Cultural Prop-

**A Meshed Celadon Flower Vase**
It is the first reported item of the Shinan Shipwreck to the government office by a local fisherman.

erties Administration formed a temporary investigation team to conduct a survey of the waters around Jeungdo Island. This turned out to be the first ever underwater survey to be conducted in the history of Korean archaeology.

The investigation identified a sunken hull containing myriad treasures. It was named the Shinan Shipwreck to commemorate the place where the ship was wrecked and ultimately discovered. The ship was found to contain countless artifacts including porcelains, metal and wooden objects, wooden tablets, medical herbs, and pieces of rosewood. Treasures that had lain buried under the seafloor for over 700 years finally recovered their rightful place in the world.

At that time, the mass media issued numerous broadcasts and

**An Unveiled Treasure Ship Discovered on the Seabed**
newspaper article dated November 1976

newspaper articles on the achievement of such an amazing excavation; and the treasure ship phenomenon began to boom throughout Korea. The excavation of the Shinan Shipwreck had given birth to underwater archaeology in Korea.

Many readers may be curious about the exact nature of the Shinan Shipwreck: What kind of ship would have contained such a huge amount of objects, and why did it sink off the coast of Shinan? This chapter should satisfy their curiosity by providing information on the date of the shipwreck, nationality, and the departure point and final destination of the ship.

## Excavation of the Shinan Shipwreck

The first excavation of the ship began in October 1976. Unfortunately, there was not a single specialist with experience of underwater excavation or even any basic survey equipment in Korea at that time. Therefore, the investigators began to conduct the survey of this ship more or less empty-handed. Furthermore, the location of the Shinan Shipwreck was not a good environment for investigation due to strong tidal currents and low visibility.

Another problem was that the investigation team could not locate the exact spot where artifacts had been collected by looters. For this reason, the investigation could only be undertaken on the basis of a statement made by an imprisoned looter. Under these circumstances, divers of the SSU(Ship Salvage Unit) of the Republic of Korea Navy conducted the investigation, while investigators of

**Excavation of the Shinan Shipwreck**
Lifting Camera on the Barge(Left), Salvaging the keel of the Shinan Shipwreck(Right)

the Cultural Properties Administration recorded the situation of the ship and the artifacts described by the divers, and classified the goods lifted from the sea.

The shipwreck was located at a point located 4 kilometers away from both Jeungdo and Imjado Islands, where strong rapid sea currents pass among the islands and the sea is characterized by dark water. The average water depth is 20 meters, with a tidal variation of 4 meters. The velocity of the tidal current is 2.5 knots per hour on average, i.e. 3.5 knots per hour during the spring tide and 1.5 knots per hour during the neap tide. The platform tide is 15 minutes. Therefore, the excavation was conducted amid a tense atmosphere around the platform tide.

Divers of the Republic of Korea Navy first installed a grid on the hull of the shipwreck, and then salvaged objects by removing mud and silt using an air lift pump. The staff of the Cultural Properties Administration produced illustrations of the deck based on conversations with the divers. A series of eleven excavations of the Shinan Shipwreck were conducted between October 1976 and September 1984.

# ● Timeline of the Excavation Survey of the Shinan Shipwreck ●

| 1976 | 1977 | 1978 | 1979 |
|---|---|---|---|
| First and Second Investigation | Third Investigation | Fourth Investigation | Fifth Investigation |

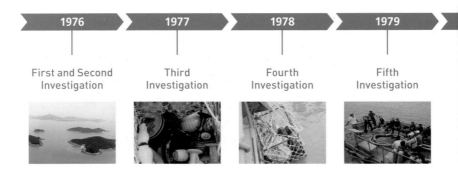

### First Investigation: 26 October to 2 November 1976

This was a preliminary investigation conducted to collect artifacts and understand the conditions of the site. A total of 112 objects including 52 celadon vessels were salvaged during the first investigation.

### Second Investigation: 9 November to 1 December 1976

As with the first investigation, the second excavation was a preliminary excavation. The investigation team salvaged 1,884 objects including 1,201 celadon vessels, and identified the buried hull. Due to the extremely cold winter weather, the full-scale excavation was begun the following year.

### Third Investigation: 27 June to 31 July 1977

With the installment of an iron grid, a full-scale underwater survey was finally undertaken, resulting in the identification of the entire shape of the shipwreck. The upper part of the hull including the deck had disappeared, and about half of the left hold was decomposed, but the right hold was more or less fully intact. Wooden boxes found under the sediment were full of porcelains, no doubt trade goods. In addition, the discovery of three Goryeo celadon vessels raised questions about the exact route of the ship.

### Fourth Investigation: 16 June to 15 August 1978

During this investigation, the wooden boxes found during the third investigation were salvaged; part of the skull of a Chinese person was identified; and many

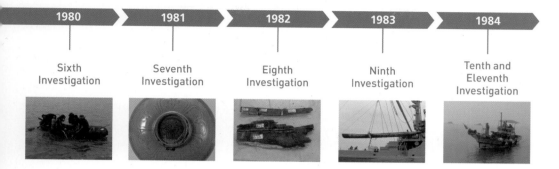

| 1980 | 1981 | 1982 | 1983 | 1984 |
|------|------|------|------|------|
| Sixth Investigation | Seventh Investigation | Eighth Investigation | Ninth Investigation | Tenth and Eleventh Investigation |

coins were identified in the port. The third and fourth excavations revealed that the hull had eight holds separated by eight bulkheads, each containing myriad objects. Bronze weights engraved with the Chinese characters 〈慶元路〉(*Qingyuanlu*), wooden tablets inscribed with the Chinese characters 〈至治參年〉(*Zhizhicannian*), and the skeletal remains of a Chinese sailor were found during this investigation.

## Fifth Investigation: 1 June to 20 July 1979

During the fifth investigation, the team investigated eight holds in a composed and orderly fashion. The pieces of rosewood were laid out on the floor, and over 28 tons of coins were placed on top of them. Due to their great weight, the bundles of coins were salvaged using air bags.

## Sixth Investigation from 5 June to 4 August 1980

During the sixth investigation, the remaining artifacts and fragmented parts of the hull were elevated before salvaging the hull.

## Seventh Investigation: 22 June to 4 August 1981

Due to its size, the entire hull could not be elevated in one go. The investigators conducted the disassembly work by sawing the hull into pieces, and the bow was salvaged. Among the many salvaged objects, the foot of a celadon bowl was found to be inscribed with the Chinese characters 〈使司帥府公用〉(*Shisishuaifgongyong*), which indicate that the bowl was produced for a local administration office of the Yuan Dynasty, thus making it possible to infer the production date contained in the hull. In addition, a lacquered dish inscribed with a pattern appeared to be the crest of an unknown Japanese house was identified, along with wooden sandals and Japanese-style pommels and sword guards.

## Eighth Investigation: 5 May to 30 September 1982

For the eighth investigation, the excavation work focused on the salvaging of the hull. It was easy enough to dismantle the bulkheads, but dragging side planks of the port and starboard was a far more difficult task. The investigators sawed side planks for salvaging, because these that were jointed with the hull by iron tenon joints measuring 7-8 centimeters long were buried under mud and silt. Since the keel measured 25 meters in length, 67 centimeters in width, and 50 centimeters in thickness, and consisted of three long wooden bars, the investigators had to disassemble two joints to salvage the keel.

## Ninth Investigation: 29 May to 25 November1983

While the salvaging of the hull continued, the last part of the keel was elevated on 21 October 1983, seven years after the first investigation

## Tenth Investigation: 1 June to 17 August 1984

In order to find any remaining objects after the salvaging of the hull, divers investigated the seafloor. In addition, the investigators dragged a cockle net across the seafloor some 40 centimeters deep to collect scattered objects. Then, the investigation team decided to finish the excavation, and removed the grid from the seafloor.

## Eleventh Investigation: 13-17 September 1984

After completing the tenth investigation, the investigation team conducted one final investigation over a period of five days. After borrowing some fishing boats, they caught forty-seven artifacts including thirty-eight celadon vessels, a rosewood object, and a fragment of the hull in fishing nets. The team was able to confirm that the ship had drifted 2 kilometers away from the initial point of the shipwreck. The investigation of the Shinan Shipwreck was finally wrapped up on 10 September 2014.

The results of the excavations of the Shinan Shipwreck were the product of the investigators' hardships and efforts. The excavation team salvaged a total of 23,502 artifacts, eight million coins(28 tons), about 1,017 pieces of rosewood, and 450 parts of the hull. As a result, Korea became the country with the largest number of porcelain objects produced during Yuan Dynasties.

Various Types of Porcelain Vessels(Left) and Coins(Right) Recovered from the Shinan Shipwreck

In fact, no one could ever have imagined that such great treasures lay buried beneath the seafloor before the discovery of the Shinan Shipwreck. The high-quality porcelains and metal objects yielded by the shipwreck attracted the public's attention; and provided the momentum for the introduction of the concept of underwater cultural heritage and the emergence of underwater archaeology as a scientific discipline in Korea.

The Gwangju National Museum was opened in 1978 to display and store the artifacts and hull structures retrieved from this shipwreck, while the Mokpo Conservation Center was established in 1981 to carry out conservation treatment of the excavated hull of the Shinan Shipwreck.

## Nationality of the Shinan Shipwreck

The Shinan Shipwreck is one of the largest medieval ships in the world to have been salvaged by underwater excavation. It is also the first sunken hull excavated in Korea; but the investigation team obtained the great achievement. There was great diversity of opinion about such issues as the nationality of the ship, the date of the shipwreck, and the purpose of the ship when the excavation began. The numerous and diverse objects(including Chinese porcelains and coins, rosewood, and medical herbs) salvaged during the long series of excavations suggested that it was a Chinese merchant vessel. Most of the recovered ceramic vessels were produced in the Longquan Kiln in Zhejiang Province and the Jingdezhen Kiln in Jiangxi Province during the Song and Yuan Periods. The fact that the ship did not contain any white and blue porcelain, which did not begin to be produced until the mid-fourteenth century, indicates that the ship was active sometime in the early fourteenth century.

Of the various types of salvaged coins, the *zhidatongbao*(至大通寶) coins cast in 1310 more clearly indicate that this was a ship of the Yuan Dynasty.

The structure of the keel explicitly demonstrates that the ship was built in China. The *baoshoukong*(保壽孔) holes made in the joints between the wooden materials in the keel are a typical feature of ships constructed in Fujian Province in China. Sailors would insert coins or bronze mirrors into these holes during ritual prayers for a safe voyage. It is known that this ritual was practiced

Plan

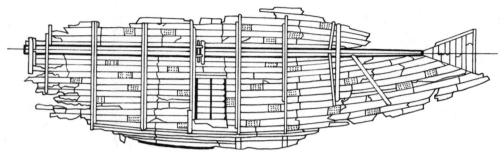

Side view

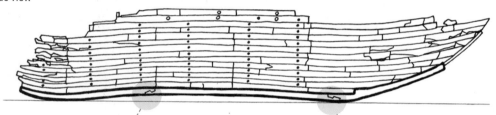

The keel of the Shinan Shipwreck: It consists of three parts, the front, main and rear parts. The joint between each part has a *baoshoukong* that is a hole for praying safe voyage.

*Taipingtongbao*(太平通寶) coins arranged in the Big Dipper Pattern in a *Baoshounkong* hole in the stern part

A bronze mirror found in a *Baoshoukong* hole in the bow part

Coins from Shinan
Shipwreck
*Xiningyuanbao*(熙
寧元寶) Coin(Left),
*Qingyuantongbao*
(慶元通寶)
Coin(Center),
*Zhidatongbao*(至大
通寶) Coins(Right)

Wooden Tablets
Written in Chinese
Characters,
*Zhizhisannian*
Wooden tablets
salvaged from the
Shinan Shipwreck
provided a clue
to the date the
ship sank. *Zhizhi*
is the era name
of Emperor
Ningzong of Yuan.
*Zhizhisannian*
means 1323 AD.

mainly in Fujian Province.

The 364 wooden tablets found in the hull provide significant information that would help to unlock the secrets of the Shinan Shipwreck. As with the wooden tablets discovered in other Korean shipwrecks, these are cargo tags recording the departure point and destination of the ship, the identity of the owners(or agencies), the shipping dates, the names(or types) and quantities(or volume) of the shipment goods, and the units of measures and weights. In particular, many tablets are inscribed with the Chinese characters <至治三年>(*zhizhisannian*), where(至治; *zhizhi*) indicates the era name of Emperor Ningzong of Yuan. Thus, zhizhisannian is 1323 AD. In addition, some cargo tags only record months and dates, such as April 22, April 23, May 11, June 1, June 2 and June 3, which suggests that the ship took on board cargos between April and June 1323.

The Shinan Shipwreck was an international trading ship of the Yuan Dynasty that navigated the seas of East Asia around 700 years ago, in other words, during the days of the Maritime Silk Road. Unfortunately, this ship whose crew perhaps imagined a new life and future prosperity was wrecked off the coast of a foreign country, taking with it the dreams of the merchants to the bottom of the sea. But this treasure ship of the Yuan Dynasty which vanished into the depths of the sea long ago has finally reappeared in our time under the name of the Shinan Shipwreck thanks to a series of underwater excavations. The salvaged hull and the objects contained in it have become time capsules that shed light on the lifestyle of merchants, trade in East Asia, and socio-economic and cultural aspects of the Medieval Period.

## The Maritime Silk Road in the Medieval Period and Sea Routes Followed by the Shinan Shipwreck

This sub-chapter explains the departure, ports of call and final destination of the Shinan Shipwreck, an international merchant vessel that navigated the Maritime Silk Road routes in the medieval period. The Shinan Ship may be viewed as a representative merchant vessel of the Maritime Silk Road in the medieval era. It measured 34 meters in length, 11 meters in width and 3.7 meters in height, had a displacement of 200 tons, and a capacity of 100 people. The relatively large size of the Shinan vessel attests to the development of shipbuilding techniques in the Song and Yuan Dynasties, and implicitly indicates the rapid progress of international trade. During that period, the boundaries of trade were extended on the back of the rapid development of nautical skills deriving from the invention of the compass in the Song Period. Whereas Chinese junks only sailed

Bronze Weight Engraved with Chinese Characters, *Qingyuanlu*

to Korea, Japan and South Asia prior to the Song Dynasty, they were able to navigate their way around the wider world in the later period. And, due to the development of ocean navigation skills, ship transports connecting East and West flourished. In addition, sailors were able to consider distinct geographical features, the flow patterns of the seas, and the tidal currents off each coast when navigating these junks.

In 1323, the Shinan Ship first shipped medicinal herbs, rosewood wares, and spices imported from South Asia at Quanzhou(泉州), one of the intermediate trade centers of the Maritime Silk Road in Fujian Province, and then sailed to Ningbo(寧波), where it took on board porcelains produced by the Longquan and Jingdezhen Kilns, before setting sail again for Hakata, its destination.

A bronze weight engraved with the Chinese characters(慶元路; *qingyuanlu*) provides definite proof of the point of the departure of the ship. Along with Guangzhou and Quanzhou, Qingyuan was one of the most important ports in southern China. The port was called Mingzhou(明州) in the Northern Song Period, Qingyuan in the Southern Song Period, and Ningbo in the Ming and Qing Periods. The government of the Song Dynasty established the *Shibósi*(市舶司), the Office of Shipping Trade, to collect tariffs and issue trading licenses.

Hakata(博多) Port in Japan was the destination of the ship. Most of the ship's cargo consisted of porcelains and coins, the main products that Japan imported from China during the Kamakura Period. Notably, wooden tablets discovered in the wreck also mention the final destinations of the cargo, including Jojeokam(釣寂庵) and the Hakojaki Shrine in Fukuoka and Tofuku-ji(東福寺) in Kyoto.

It is assumed that the Japanese owners or agents of the shipment were on board. The wooden sandals, Japanese chess pieces and Japanese-type sword-guards founding the ship validate this hypothesis. In addition, the bronze spoons recovered from the hull indicate that the ship was also manned by Korean sailors.

There are two broad opinions about the routes taken by the Shinan Ship. The first view is that the ship took the direct sea route between China and Japan, with Hakata Port in Japan as its final destination. Before the fourteenth century, it was dangerous to sail directly across the East China Sea. Therefore, ships travelling from China to Japan usually sailed north up the east coast of China to the Shandong Peninsula, and then south along the west coast of

Wooden Tablet Inscribed with the name "Tofuku-ji," the Final Destination of the Cargos on the Shinan Ship

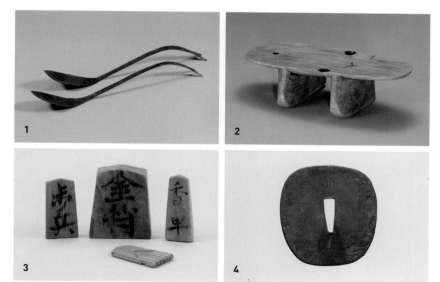

1 Bronze Spoon
2 Wooden Sandal
3 Japanese Chess Pieces
4 Sword-guard

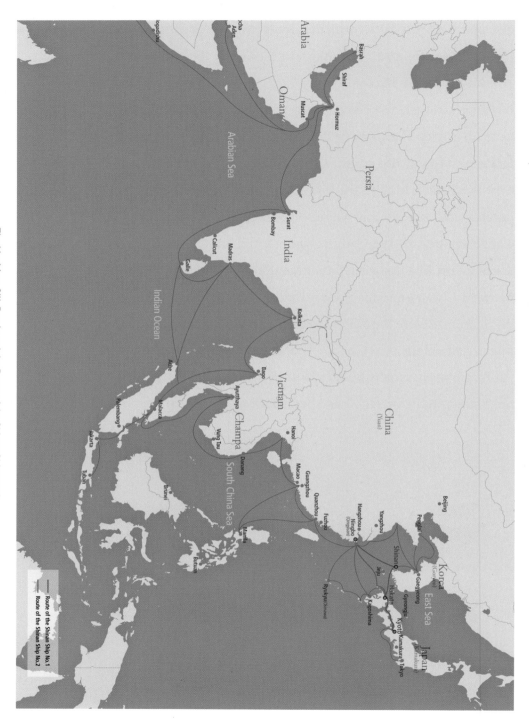

The Maritime Silk Roads and the Route of the Shinan Shipwreck

Route of the Shinan Ship No.1
Route of the Shinan Ship No.2

Korea. Due to the development of nautical skills in the fourteenth century, ships could follow the direct route between China and Japan by taking advantage of the prevailing southeast wind in May and June on the lunar calendar. It seems that the Shinan Ship ran into a storm near Jeju Island after departing from Ningbo, causing it to drift along the coast of Shinan where it finally sank.

The second view holds that the Shinan Shipwreck must have sailed from Qingyuan to Japan via Goryeo. Assuming that the Shinan Ship was blown off course, the point where it sank is too far away from the direct sea route across the East China Sea. Moreover, this point is located on the route taken by the ship that carried Xu Jing, an envoy of the Song Dynasty, to the Goryeo capital of Gaegyeong.

Although it has not yet been confirmed which route the Shinan Ship took, the cause of the shipwreck is very clear. The ship struck a rock or a reef. When the hull of this ship was discovered, its bow was oriented 323 degrees northwest, and its hull, which lay buried under mud, had a starboard list of 15 degrees. The underwater excavation revealed the broken side planks of the right side that bent inside of the hull, and wooden fragments scattered around the hull. In order to protect the hull under the load line, the side strakes of the Shinan Ship, a large merchant vessel, put wooden boards. Moreover, flooding of the entire hull could be prevented by locking the drainage lines installed between the bulkheads. However, the Shinan ship and its crew were sent to the bottom of the sea in an instant by a tragic accident.

## Significant Shipments on the Shinan Ship

The remains of the cargos discovered in and outside the hull of the Shinan Ship provided invaluable data that shed light on medieval trade networks and goods. They are highly significant in that they corroborate the maritime silk route in Northeast Asia during the medieval period.

Most of the porcelains found on the ship were products of the Song and Yuan Dynasties. From the ninth to the nineteenth century porcelain wares were special products of China that were exported to Asia, Europe, Africa and the Mediterranean Sea. They were also the main trade good transported along the Maritime Silk Road routes. The porcelains of the Shinan Shipwreck clearly illustrate the active trade policy of the Yuan Dynasty and the marine trade networks around the fourteenth century.

An impressive 20,660 porcelain vessels produced at various kiln sites in China were salvaged from the underwater excavation of the Shinan site. Indeed, the ship's main cargos consisted of celadon vessels from the Longquan Kiln in Zhejiang Province, white porcelains from the Jingdezhen Kiln, white glaze and underglaze black painted vessels from the Jizhouyao Kiln in Jiangxi Province, and black glazed vessels from the Jianyao Kiln in Fujian Province. In addition, the ship was loaded with porcelain vessels produced at various kilns in Jiangsu, Guangdong and Hebei Provinces.

The celadon vessels fired at the Longquan Kiln(about 12,000 items including dishes, bowls, stands, ewers, incense burners, flower vases and human figurines) account for the majority of the ceramic vessels salvaged from the wreck. Notably, the celadon vase caught along with a webfoot octopus by a fisherman is a product of the Longquan Kiln. The Shinan Shipwreck contained many flower vases because Japanese people of the Kamakura Period greatly appreciated vases filled with flowers.

Meanwhile, black glazed tea bowls fired at the Jianyao Kiln were a popular item in the Song Period. The Shinan Ship yielded sixty of these black glazed tea bowls, which were highly appreciated by the Japanese, who called them *temmoku*(天目).

In addition, the shipwreck contained seven pieces of Goryeo celadon, including a prunus vase, a bowl, a cupstand, a pillow and a water dropper produced at the Sadang-ri Kiln in Gangjin and the Yucheon-ri Kiln in Buan from the thirteenth to fourteenth centuries. It seems that these goods were loaded in China, which gives an idea of the complex nature of the international trade network at that time, when Goryeo celadon was famous for its beautiful color.

In addition to these ceramic vessels, the ship was carrying more than eight million Chinese coins weighing about 28 tons and ranging from the Xin to Yuan Periods, as well as Vietnamese coins. It seems that the Japanese imported them either for use as currency or in the casting of Buddha statues, which were produced in great quantities during the Kamakura Period. An analysis of the components of the Great Buddha of Kamakura detected elements contained in Chinese coins.

Rosewood, which grows widely throughout South East Asia,

including Sri Lanka and Indonesia, has heavy, yellow, and fine-grained tissues, for which reason it was used to produce high-quality furniture, art works and statues of Buddha. The Shinan Ship contained rosewood logs and incense made from the wood of this tree. It seems that the Shinan Ship loaded up with these goods in Quanzhou, a port located south of Qingyuan. These items are inscribed not only with Chinese characters indicating the identities of their owners, but also with inscriptions in Roman and Arabic numerals which appear to have been engraved by European and Arabic merchants, and figures such as circles and triangles.

In addition to ceramic vessels, coins, and rosewood objects, the ship yielded various goods made of metal, wood, stone, and

Goryeo Celadon
Vessels from the
Shinan Shipwreck

**Porcelains from Shinan Shipwreck**

1 Celadon Dish with Plum Blossom Design (Longquan Kiln)
2 Celadon Jar with Five Spouts (Longquan Kiln)
3 Celadon Vase with Fishlike Dragon Handle (Longquan Kiln)
4 Black Glazed Bowl(Jianyao Kiln)
5 White Porcelain Dish with Plum Blossom Design (Jingdezhen Kiln)
6 White Porcelain Bottle with Two Handles and Plum Blossom Design (Jingdezhen Kiln)
7 Long-necked Bottle with White Glaze and Underglaze Black Painted Wave and Floral Design (Jizhouyao Kiln)

**Rosewood**
These objects are inscribed with Chinese characters, Roman letters and other symbols.

tin(which was in various alloys) ingots. The wine goblet, called a *gu*(觚) in Chinese, recovered from the hull was an imitation of an item produced in the Shang Period, and was probably destined for use as a flower vase. Among the recovered wooden vessels are lacquered bowls and jars, while tea leaf grinding stone and bird-shaped ink-stones are among the most significant stone goods salvaged from the site. The hull also contained spices imported from South Asia, including peppers, cinnamon bark, and clove buds, and seeds of lychees produced in southern China. Medicinal herbs and spices were probably trade goods but they could just as easily have been emergency medicines for the ship's crew.

In order to cross the sea shipped with so many different goods, the ship's crew carefully stacked them in the hull. Coins were placed on heavy rosewood logs that were themselves laid on the narrow bottom to spread the weight evenly and use the limited space more efficiently. Wooden boxes contained precious and expensive goods, including porcelain vessels, lacquered objects and metal goods, were stacked neatly on top of the coins to prevent them from being damaged.

**Artifacts from Shinan Shipwreck**

1 Lacquered Bowl
2 Lacquered Jar with Peony Design
3 Bird-shaped Ink-stone
4 Millstone
5 Bronze Boshan-shaped Incense Burner
6 Tin Ingots
7 Tin Wine Goblet
8 Glass Hairpins and Beads
9 Lychee Seeds

# Anheungryang in Taean, the "Bermuda Triangle" of Korea

Chapter 4

# Anheungryang in Taean, the "Bermuda Triangle" of Korea

The entirety of the Taean Peninsula, which is famous for its beautiful islands and beaches, was designated as a National Park in 1978. However, unlike its common name of Taean, which means "peace"(泰) and "comfort"(安), the coastal region of Taean has long been notorious for its dangerous marine environment as countless ships were wrecked in the seawaters during the Goryeo and Joseon Periods. As in the legend of the beautiful maiden named Lorelei who sat on a rock and enchanted sailors with her beauty, leading them to crash their ships into the rocks or run aground in shallow water, perhaps sailors were lured by the scenic landscapes of Taean, causing them to sail their ships into the dangerous rocks along the Taean coastline.

The marine environment of this stretch of the Korean coast is characterized by strong offshore drifts and rocky reefs; thus a ship could be wrecked in an instant if its crew failed to concentrate. Due to its rough waterway, Anheungryang, the name of the strait around Mado and Sinjindo Islands, the western end of Taean-gun County is even called "the Bermuda Triangle of Korea."

Along with Uldolmok in Jindo, which is well known as the site of the Battle of Myeongnang, Sondolmok in Ganghwado Island, which is notorious for its fast currents, and Indangsu in Hwanghae-do Province, the setting for the story of Simcheong, this coastal region is one of the four roughest sea routes in Korea. The place name "Anheungryang" clearly attests to

**Gwanjangmok**
The northern end of Anheungryang is called "Gwanjangmok" or "Gwansugwak."

ancient fears about this dangerous sea route. Anheungryang was known by various other names including Anhaengryang(安行梁), Anhangryang(安恒梁), and Anhaengdo(安行渡). According to *Sinjeung donggukyeoji seungram*(新增東國輿地勝覽), a geography book published during the Joseon Dynasty,

> This(place) was called Nanhaengryang(難行梁) in the past, but as the name was unpopular because many cargo vessels had been wrecked on this rough sea route, the local people gave it its current name.

'Nanhaeng,' which means "rough voyage," is a name that clearly refers to the rugged nature of this sea, which poses a serious obstacle to safe navigation. Nevertheless, people who observed

Rocks off the Coast of Mado Island

the tragic accidents in the area must have found the name disagreeable as they changed it to Anheungryang, which roughly means 'standing up safely,' representing their wishes for a safe voyage.

So why was this sea so dangerous? Xu Jing, an envoy of the Song Dynasty who stayed at Anheungjeong (安興亭) Inn on Mado Island in 1123 AD, described the situation as the ship he was traveling on passed Anheungryang in his book *Xuanhe Fengshi Gaoli Tujing*(宣和奉使高麗圖經):

> Rocks protruding from the sea cause a strong backwash. The strangely rushing rapids are beyond description. Sailors dare not attempt to approach the rapids for fear of running the ship onto the reef.

According to *Sinjeung donggukyeoji seungram*(新增東國輿地勝覽):

> Several currents collide with each other off the coast of Anheungjeong. In addition, there are several dangerous points caused by the reefs. Together these elements have caused several ships to capsize...

Even now, the reefs mentioned in historical sources can be easily identified. The rocks that are submerged at high tide and exposed at low tide pose a threat to ships. Moreover, the topography of the region, which is characterized by complex shorelines and

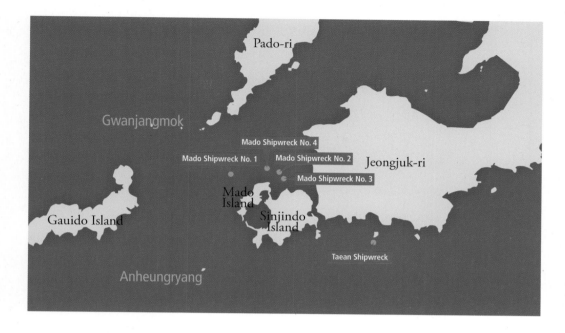

Map labels: Pado-ri, Gwanjangmok, Mado Shipwreck No. 4, Mado Shipwreck No. 1, Mado Shipwreck No. 2, Jeongjuk-ri, Mado Shipwreck No. 3, Mado Island, Gauido Island, Sinjindo Island, Taean Shipwreck, Anheungryang

numerous islands, causes rapid variations in the course and velocity of the tidal currents, making sailing even more difficult. In addition, the Taean Peninsula projects from the coast and is enveloped with heavy fog during spring and summer. All these environmental factors threaten the safe passage of ships in this region.

Anheungryang and the Investigated Points of Shipwrecks

## Attempts to Construct a Canal

Such adverse environmental conditions in Anheungryang were a source of great distress for the government in the Goryeo and Joseon Periods, as cargo vessels transporting taxes—including goods and grains collected in places south of Chungcheong-do Province—to the royal capital were frequently wrecked in this strait. For example, during a period of sixty years from the fourth year of King Taejo's reign(1395 AD) to the first year of King Sejo's reign(1455 AD), about 200 cargo vessels were destroyed or sank in Anheungryang, with the loss of 1,200 sailors and more than 15,800 *seoks*(石) of grain.

In order to prevent further maritime accidents, several attempts were made to construct a canal in the Goryeo and Joseon Periods. The history of Gulpo Canal, which began to be constructed in the twelfth year of King Injong of Goryeo(1134 AD), is typical of such efforts. It was planned to connect Cheonsuman Bay in Taean with Garorimman Bay in Seosan(approx. 6.8 km in length). After digging a water course about 4 kilometers long, the construction work was interrupted when the solid bedrock layer was struck. Work on the canal was resumed in the third year of King Gongyang of Goryeo(1391 AD), without success, and was finally abandoned in the twelfth year of King Taejong of Joseon(1412 AD)as the channel was too narrow and too shallow, making it impossible for cargo vessels containing about 500 *seoks* of grain to pass through it. Although small vessels with a cargo of about 150 *seoks* of grain could pass through it, it eventually fell into

**Canals in the Taean Area**

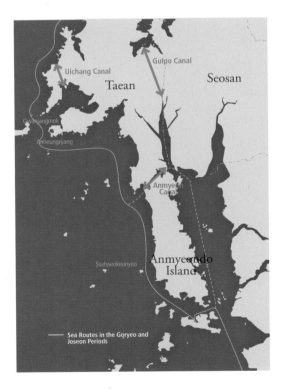

86

disuse due to silt deposits. The Joseon royal court made another attempt to build the Gulpo Canal in the reign of King Sejo of Joseon, before finally abandoning the plan altogether.

The Uihang Canal connecting Uihang-ri with Mohang-ri in Taean was built during the reign of King Jungjong of Joseon; while the construction of the Anmyeon Canal in the reign of King Injo of Joseon transformed Anmyeondo, which was originally a peninsula projecting from Taean, into an island. However, these two canals were not efficient channels for the transportation of goods because ships still had to pass via Anheungryang in order to use them.

## Taean Shipwreck, a Treasure Ship Laden with Goryeo Celadon Vessels

In 1131, a cargo vessel fully laden with batches of Goryeo celadon set sail from Gangjin. The ship followed the sea route off the coast of Jeollanam-do Province, and cruised along the West Sea coast in Chungcheong-do Province. The ship would then have continued to Gyeonggi-do Province in accordance with its schedule after passing Anheungryang between Sinjindo and Mado Islands.

However, the ship sank in the deep waters off the coast of an uninhabited island called Daeseom. Was the ship overloaded with too many goods or did its crew fail to detect a reef due to heavy fog? The one fact that we know with any certainty is that the ship was swept along by strong currents upon reaching the entrance to

**Goryeo White Porcelain Case**
This is the only Goryeo white porcelain found in a Goryeo shipwreck.

**Illustration of the Taean Shipwreck**
This is the third layer of batches of Goryeo celadon vessels, which were placed in the hull lying east-west.

Anheungryang. The ship sank to the bottom of the sea along with all its crew and its precious cargo.

The heroine of this tragic accident lay submerged underwater for 900 years, and was only discovered and ultimately salvaged when a fisherman caught a celadon bowl along with a webfoot octopus. This is the Taean Shipwreck, thus named to commemorate the place where the ship was found.

The Taean Shipwreck was well preserved under the sea because the area in which it sank was designated as a military protection zone in the 1970s. This ship contained more than 25,000 Goryeo celadon vessels, most of which are dishes and bowls, although other precious relics including a toad-shaped ink-stone and a li-

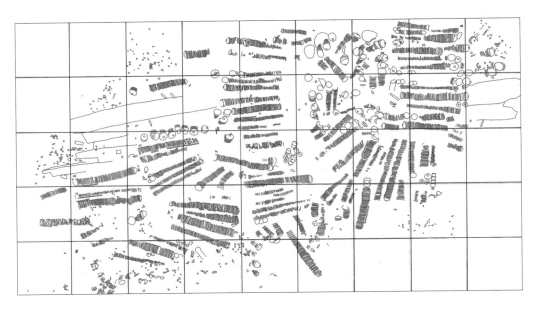

onshaped incense burner were also salvaged from the wreck. These celadon vessels were stacked up on the deck in five layers: High-grade vessels, including *balwoo* and dishes with lotus petals design were placed at the center of the hull; while low-graded vessels were stacked in the bow and stern of the ship.

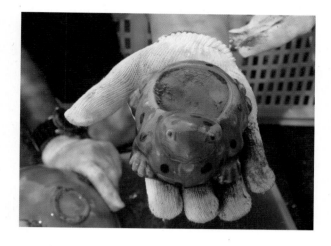

Toad-shaped Ink-stone

A Goryeo white porcelain case, the first one ever found in an underwater survey in Korea, aroused the investigators' curiosity. They tried to find its lid, without success. Shards of celadon vessels, which were moved by the tidal currents, were found clustered in one point of the investigated area. The excavators salvaged them at a time. While classifying them on the barge, the investigators found a toad-shaped celadon ink-stone. Therefore, there is no photo of this object taken in the underwater.

In addition, the wooden tablets recovered from the ship were a source of surprise and wonder to all the researchers who saw them. Prior to the discovery of the Taean Shipwreck, only the Shinan Shipwreck, a ship of the Yuan Dynasty that was wrecked off the coast of Shinan, had yielded up such wooden tablets. Therefore, it was difficult to obtain precise information about the sunken ship, such as its departure and destination points or the date on which it sank. The contents written on the wooden tablets

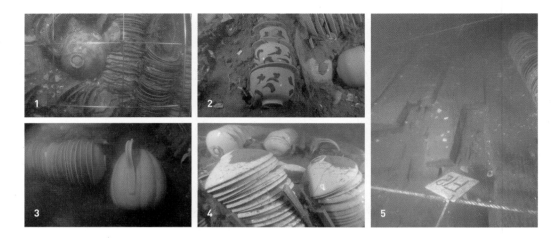

suggest that the Taean Ship was a celadon carrier that sailed from Gangjin to Gaegyeong, its final destination.

## Discovery in the Mado Sea, a Treasure Trove of Underwater Cultural Heritage in Korea

The wreck of the Taean Ship was not the last tragic accident to occur in Anheungryang. In 2007, when the investigation team was busy conducting an excavation(survey) of the Taean Shipwreck off the coast of Daeseom Island, a local fisherman reported the discovery of twenty-four celadon vessels in three fishing nets. In fact, these were vestiges of another tragic accident. Immediately upon receiving the report, the investigation team conducted an exploration of the seafloor; but it was impossible to survey the reported point as kelp farms had been established in this area, and diving under them was dangerous due to the many ropes and anchors installed to build kelp farms. However, the institute

decided to investigate the area inside the kelp farms in May and July 2008, and uncovered three batches of celadon vessels.(A batch consists of fifty celadon vessels wrapped in straw ropes for one person to carry; a rope bundles up three bunches.) Apart from these celadon vessels, the survey team did not find any other objects such as ceramic vessels or parts of the hull.

In March 2009, the investigation team on board the Sea Muse began to survey the northern sector some 1.3 kilometers away from the point where the batches of celadon vessels had previously been salvaged. This is a dangerous sea to navigate due to the presence of reefs; and the underwater environment there is very poor due to low visibility. One diver came up from the water with celadon vessels and an iron caldron containing white porcelain vessels that he found on the seafloor without observation. Iron caldrons were used by sailors to cook food, and have been frequently found in underwater surveys.

Therefore, the investigation team regarded the iron caldron as a clue to finding the shipwreck, and waited for a better underwater environment before conducting a full-scale survey in this area

Batches of Goryeo Celadon Vessels Found off the Coast of Mado Island(Left), Iron Caldron from the North to the Sea of Mado Island(Right)

from April 27, 2009. The investigators identified myriad porcelains including celadon, white porcelain, and Chinese porcelain scattered over a vast area of the seafloor in subsequent surveys.

Immediately afterward, the survey team found parts of the hull of Mado Shipwreck No. 1, which sank in the Goryeo Period, and then conducted an excavation of the shipwreck. At the same time, the Institute was also conducting a survey of this sea, and found two Goryeo shipwrecks, Mado Shipwrecks Nos. 2 and 3, in 2009. These were excavated in 2010 and 2011, respectively, while Mado Shipwreck No. 4, a Joseon ship discovered in 2014, was excavated in 2015.

The underwater survey of the Sea of Mado, under way since 2009, has led us to think that many more sunken hulls may still be hidden under the mud in this area, making it the most significant underwater site in Korean underwater archaeology.

## Mado Shipwreck No. 1, the First Grain Carrier Ever Discovered in Korean Waters

Rice and Rice Bags(Left), Soybean(Center) and Buckwheat (Right) from Mado Shipwreck No. 1

In 2007, the Sea Muse explored a point of the seabed near a reef off Mado Island where various objects were(located) densely buried

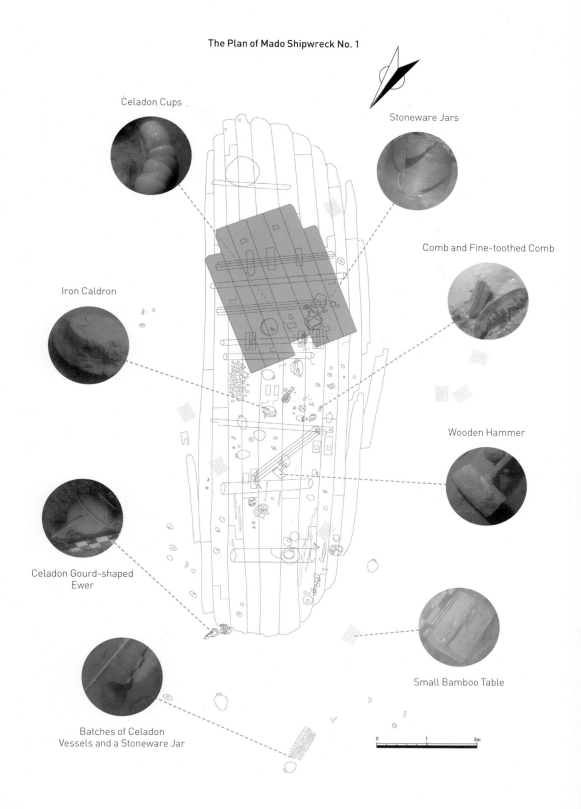

# The Plan of Mado Shipwreck No. 1

Celadon Cups

Stoneware Jars

Comb and Fine-toothed Comb

Iron Caldron

Wooden Hammer

Celadon Gourd-shaped
Ewer

Small Bamboo Table

Batches of Celadon
Vessels and a Stoneware Jar

0    1    2m

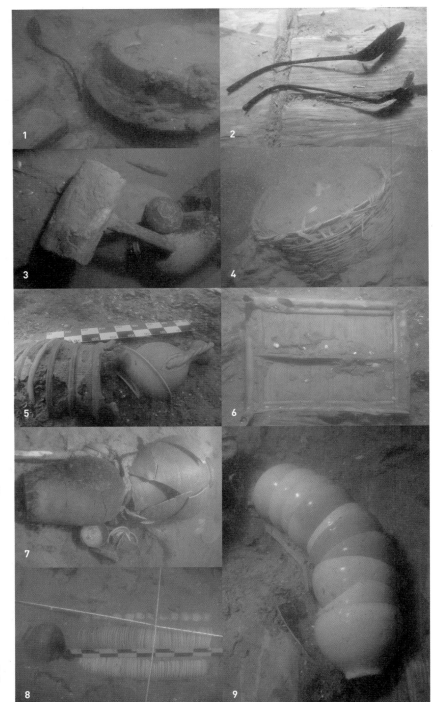

**Artifacts in Mado Shipwreck No. 1**

1 Iron Caldron and a Bronze Spoon
2 Bronze Spoons
3 Wooden Hammer
4 Bamboo Basket
5 Celadon Gourd-shaped Ewer, Saucer and Pottery Stands
6 Small Bamboo Table
7 Stoneware Jars
8 Batches of Celadon Vessels and a Stoneware Jar
9 Celadon Cups

under silt. Wooden logs rising above the seafloor were detected on May 5. These were parts of the hull. The next day, divers identified a hull with three decks. This was Mado Shipwreck No. 1, another victim of Anheungryang.

Unlike the Taean Shipwreck, which was heavily loaded with porcelain vessels, Mado Shipwreck No. 1 was found to be full of grains, making it the first grain carrier ship ever discovered in Korea. The ship contained various grains including rice, millet, buckwheat, and beans, and stoneware jars containing salted fermented foods made with mackerel and crab. Only rice hulls were remaining. Bags and wooden tablets seemed to be tags attached to bags were identified. The ship was also carrying other cargos such as celadon lidded cups, a gourd-shaped celadon ewer with an inlaid peony design, celadon vases with an underglaze iron design.

The bow of the hull was severely decomposed. Batches of celadon vessels and nine small bamboo trays were found scattered around the hull. These distribution patterns suggest that the bow, which was broken apart by the shock of colliding with the reef, was driven into the hull; and that much of the cargo stored in the hull fell into the sea as the ship was sinking.

In addition, a very small fragment of a wooden object inscribed with Chinese characters raised the possibility that this shipwreck contained wooden tablets, as with the Taean Shipwreck. Therefore, the investigation team conducted the excavation very carefully. After completing the investigation of the inside of the hull, six wooden tablets were found under the bottom planks. These are inscribed with the words: "Your sincerely, sending six bags of rice to the House of *Daejanggun*(Great General) Kim Sunyeong(金純永)." On the basis of the person's name, Kim Sunyeong, who appears in historical sources, the researchers were able to reveal the date the ship sank and the overall characteristics of the shipwreck. Comprehensive studies of the Chinese characters written on the wooden tablets indicate that the ship was loaded with rice, millet and buckwheat in Haenam, Naju and Jangheung in Jeolla-do Province between October 1207 and February 1208, in order to transport them to Gaegyeong, before it sank in the waters off Mado Island.

## Mado Shipwreck No. 2, Carrier Containing Celadon Prunus Vases

In early October 2009, when the underwater excavation of Mado Shipwreck No. 1 was nearing its end, and while a barge was conducting a preliminary excavation about 1 kilometer east of the barge that was carrying out the underwater excavation of Mado Shipwreck No. 1, a diver seeking objects in the trench dug on the seafloor sent a message to the investigators on the barge.

> I have glimpsed some wooden logs with bark and porcelain
> vessels. Having poked into the gap between the wooden logs,
> it seems that more porcelain vessels are lying there.

For the investigators who had been silently conducting investigations over a period of several months in the hope of finding more objects, this was very happy and exciting news. As they removed silt and mud from the seafloor, a part of the hull and shards of a celadon prunus vase were exposed. This was Mado Shipwreck No. 2.

A full-scale underwater excavation of this ship was undertaken in 2010. The discovery of shards of prunus vases in the 2009 investigation raised the possibility that the ship contained more of them. As expected, two beautiful celadon prunus vases were found lying side by side beneath the sediment. These two vessels were each attached with a wooden cargo tag recording the goods contained in them, i.e. honey and sesame oil, respectively.

The characters on the wooden tablets clearly show that the ship was a cargo vessel that was transporting grains collected in local provinces to government officials in Gaegyeong. The ship contained more than 400 objects including various types of grain, its

**Seabed Image of the Mado Sea Produced by a Multi-beam Eco Sounder**
The areas where sediment was removed in the preliminary excavation are marked by long and short lines. The blue circle indicates Mado Shipwreck No. 2.

# The Plan of Mado Shipweck No. 2

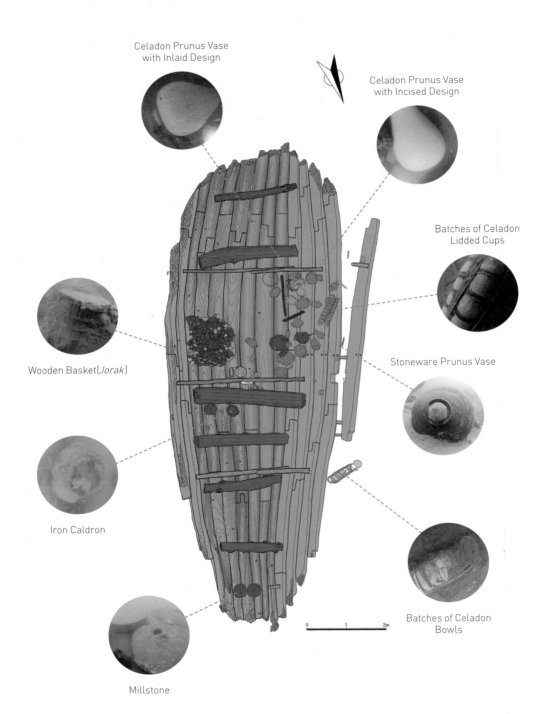

Celadon Prunus Vase
with Inlaid Design

Celadon Prunus Vase
with Incised Design

Batches of Celadon
Lidded Cups

Wooden Basket(*Jorak*)

Stoneware Prunus Vase

Iron Caldron

Batches of Celadon
Bowls

Millstone

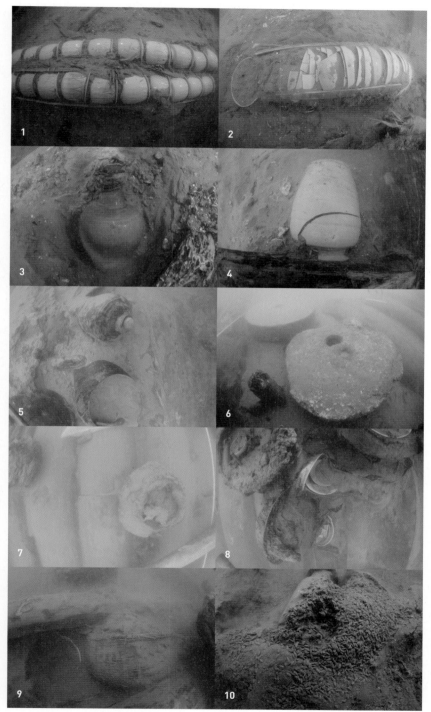

**Artifacts in Mado Shipwreck No. 2**

1 Batches of Celadon Lidded Cups
2 Batches of Celadon Bowls
3 Celadon Vase
4 Celadon Jar
5 Stoneware Prunus Vase and a Stoneware Jar
6 Millstone
7 Iron Caldron
8 Iron Caldrons and Other Objects
9 Bamboo Basket
10 Rice Seeds

main cargo, ceramic vessels such as celadon dishes, prunus vases, and lidded cups, wooden tablets(cargo tags), animal bones, and sailors' possessions such as iron caldrons, bronze spoons, bronze bowls, and bamboo chopsticks.

Studies on the names of the people recorded on the wooden tablets revealed that the ship was wrecked sometime before 1213 AD.


## Mado Shipwreck No. 3, a Ship Transporting Cargos to Powerful Men

On September 12, one month before the identification of Mado Shipwreck No. 2, the Sea Muse found another ship, Mado Shipwreck No. 3, in shallow sea just 300 meters from coastline. The excavation campaign of this ship was undertaken in 2011.

According to the contents of the wooden tablets, the ship was loaded in Jeollanam-do Province and destined for Ganghwado Island, the temporary capital of Goryeo. Unlike Mado Shipwreck Nos. 1 and 2 which were shipping private goods to officials serving in government institutes, this ship was transporting goods for a certain Kim Jun, the most powerful man in the Goryeo court, his men, and his private institutions.

The cargos loaded on this ship differed markedly from those carried by Mado Shipwreck Nos. 1 and 2. Among the items salvaged from the wreck were bamboo boxes containing shark bones(found in the stern); a wooden tablet containing the following

# The Plan of Mado Shipwreck No. 3

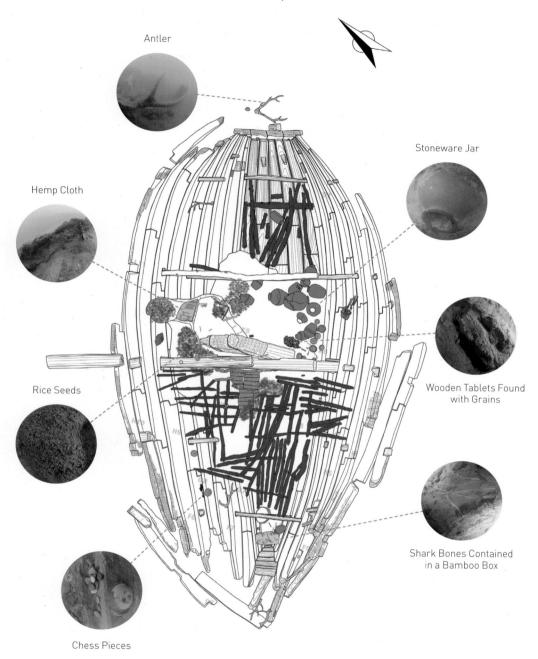

Antler

Stoneware Jar

Hemp Cloth

Rice Seeds

Wooden Tablets Found
with Grains

Shark Bones Contained
in a Bamboo Box

Chess Pieces

**Artifacts in Mado Shipwreck No. 3**
1 Bronze Bell
2 Chess Pieces
3 Cockle Shell Written with Chinese Characters
4 Antlers
5 Hemp Cloth
6 Rice Seeds
7 Barley Seeds and a Bag
8 Stoneware Jar
9 Stoneware Jar Containing River Gravels
10 Bronze Vessels

Stoneware Jars
and Bottles from
Mado Shipwreck
No. 3

record: "Sending sharks contained in box to *Doryeong*(都領) of *Usambyeolcho*(右三別抄)"; a wooden tablet containing the record "Sending 15 rolls of hemp cloths to *Dogwan*(都官) put on grain bags; and wooden tablets containing a record of various types of cargos, including dog meat jerky, abalones, mussels, and fish oil. Except for the celadon vessels used as utensils by the ship's crew, there were no celadon vessels on this ship. Unusually, the ship contained forty-five stoneware jars, most of which contained salted fermented fish; while a few jars served as food and water containers for the sailors. The hull also contained various items used by the crew including bronze bowls, spoons and chopsticks; while chess pieces made of smooth pebbles give us an inkling of how the ship's crew spent their leisure time on board the ship. In addition, twelve antlers were found inside and around the hull. It has been suggested that these were raw materials used in the production of art objects or styptics, although their actual purpose has not yet been determined.

Of the shipwrecks excavated in Korea, the hull of this ship was in the best condition. Five rows of the bottom plank, nine levels of the starboard, and ten levels of the port were preserved under mud and silt. Although the hulls of the other shipwrecks were disassembled for salvaging, the Institute decided to bury the hull of this ship after completing its investigations and to wait for better salvaging technology to be developed.

## Mado Shipwreck No. 4, a Cargo Vessel of the Joseon Period

In 2014, the Nurian began conducting the preliminary excavation in the Sea of Mado, but was replaced by the Sea Muse in early September due to a problem with her generator. A wooden anchor and wooden materials that appeared to be broken parts of the hull were detected in October; and bundles of white porcelains were found in a spot about 30 meters away from the hull fragments. This marked the discovery of Mado Shipwreck No. 4.

At the beginning of the investigation of the hull, the investigators assumed that the ship contained white porcelain vessels, but their assumption proved to be incorrect. While they were removing the sediment, they were watching the hull loaded with *buncheong* vessels produced in the early fifteenth century. The investigators were puzzled by the discovery in the hull of *buncheong* ware vessels that were produced 400 years earlier than the white

# The Plan of Mado Shipwreck No. 4

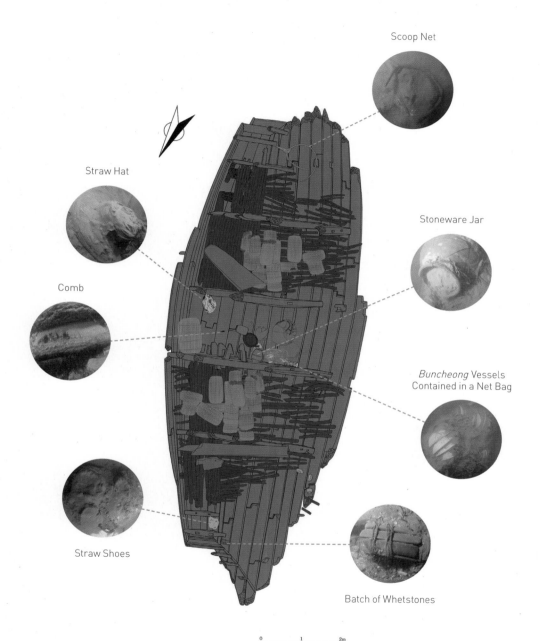

Scoop Net

Straw Hat

Comb

Stoneware Jar

*Buncheong* Vessels
Contained in a Net Bag

Straw Shoes

Batch of Whetstones

0    1    2m

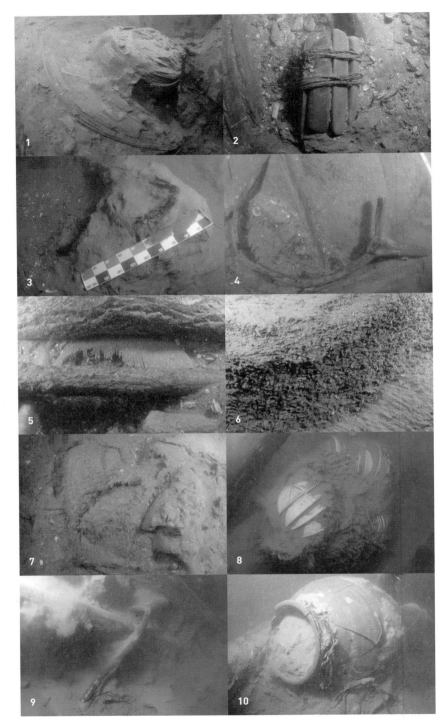

**Artifacts in Mado Shipwreck No. 4**

1 Straw Hat
2 Batch of Whetstones
3 Straw Shoes
4 Scoop Net
5 Comb
6 Rice Seeds
7 Net Bag
8 *Buncheong* Vessels Contained in a Net Bag
9 Adze Haft
10 Stoneware Jar

porcelain vessels found in the preliminary excavation. Due to the unusually low winter temperature, the investigators had to wait six months to have an opportunity to solve this puzzle. The excavation resumed in 2015.

The underwater excavation of the ship revealed 155 *buncheong* ware vessels but no white porcelain vessels. Therefore, the results of the excavation suggest that the bundles of white porcelain vessels salvaged in the preliminary excavation were not part of the cargo of this ship. If that was the case, then why were the white porcelain vessels buried at a spot near the hull of Mado Shipwreck No. 4?

One hypothesis is as follows: 400 years after Mado Shipwreck No. 1, bundles of white porcelain vessels loaded on a ship that was in danger of sinking accidentally fell into the water at this point. Given that lots of marine accidents happened in this coastal region, this is the most plausible assumption.

As with other shipwrecks excavated in the area, wooden tablets recovered from this ship played a crucial role in revealing the characteristics of this shipwreck. Of many wooden tablets, 54 were inscribed with the word Najugwangheungchang. Here, Naju(羅州) refers to present-day Naju in Jeollanam-do Province, while Gwangheungchang(廣興倉) refers to a tax storehouse of the Joseon Period that also paid a stipend to officials. The Gwangheungchang located in present-day Mapo in Seoul was the final destination of all tax carriers during the Joseon Period. In addition to the grains paid as taxes, the shipped items consisted of tribute payments to the government and the royal court, including *buncheong* wares and whetstones, and goods for the crew members, such as straw hats and shoes, adzes, and scoops. According to *Sinjeung donggukyeoji seungram*, whetstones were a special product of Naju, the point of departure of this ship. Therefore, these items seem to be tributary payments.

## The Sea of Mado, a Port of Call on the Shipping Route

The wrecks of four ships that were carrying ceramic vessels such as celadon, white porcelain, stoneware and Chinese porcelain, bronze spoons, iron caldrons, and anchor stones have been salvaged from the sea of Mado, providing definite evidence that

Chinese Characters Written on the Bottom of Chinese Porcelain Vessels Found in the Sea off Mado Island

this coast was a busy sea route in ancient times.

More than 200 Chinese porcelain vessels were recovered from the bottom of the sea of Mado in 2009-2012. Most of them are white porcelain vessels; but several items of black-glaze celadon and stoneware vessels were also salvaged. These ceramic vessels were produced at kilns in southern China, in-

Stoneware Jars with Four Lugs Salvaged from the Sea off Mado Island
These objects prove that trade and exchanges took place between Goryeo and the Yuan Dynasty.

cluding Fujian, Zhejiang, Jiangxi, Jiangsu and Guangdong Provinces, during the Song and Yuan Periods. One of the most important facts is that the feet of many of the porcelain vessels are inscribed with Chinese characters. *Zheng Gang*(鄭綱), *Yang Gang*(楊綱) and *Lin Gang*(林綱) are composed of a letter indicating surnames(鄭, 楊 and 林) and a letter *gang*(綱). The bottom of several vessels contains only a surname, signature or the character *gang*(綱). In general, porcelain vessels inscribed with the Chinese character *gang*(綱) have been found in international trade vessels from the Song Dynasty. In addition, jars with four lugs, called monggobyeong(Mongolian bottles), that show the trade network of the Yuan Dynasty. This type of vessel was also part of the shipment of the Shinan Shipwreck, an international trade vessel of the Yuan Dynasty.

The fact that many objects related with Chinese merchants have been discovered in this part of the sea suggests that Chinese merchants who were bound for Gaegyeong, the capital of Goryeo, stayed on Mado Island. According to *Xuanhe Fengshi Gaoli Tujing*:

> The ship quickly dropped anchor off the coast of Mado Island... An inn there is called *Anheungjeong*(安興亭)... The envoy came ashore on a small boat... I declined an invitation to a banquet, and returned to the ship at midnight.

This record clearly indicates that Xu's party, which was headed for Gaegyeong, stayed overnight in this area. The record and the artifacts salvaged from the seafloor suggest that Mado was a port of call between the Song Dynasty and Gaegyeong. Not only international trade vessels, but all manner of ships, including Mado Shipwreck Nos. 1, 2, 3 and 4, that passed Anheungryang may have stayed here.

The coastal environment of this region made the sea of Mado Island a port of call. In order to arrive at Gaegyeong or Hanyang, ships that sailed along the coast from south had to pass via Gwanjangmok to the north of Mado Island. Due to the strong and rough currents around Gwanjangmok, sailing vessels that navigated the sea using tidal currents and wind power could not easily pass by Gwanjangmok during ebb tide when the tidal currents flow from north to south and reefs are exposed above the surface of the water. Therefore, the ship was waiting for the flood tide in the sea of Mado. Moreover, the northeast area of this sea

**Anchor Stones**
These demonstrate that various types of ships dropped anchor in the sea off Mado Island.

was the best place for ships to drop anchor, because Mado Island would have shielded them from the southerly wind that blows strongly in spring and summer.

The 130 or so anchor stones salvaged in this area also demonstrate that the ship had to sail in the sea of Mado to pass Gwanjangmok. Anchor stones of various sizes ranging from 40 centimeters to more than 200 centimeters in length, and from 5 kilograms to more than 1,000 kilograms in weight, were salvaged from this sea, which demonstrates that various types of ships dropped anchor in the waters off Mado Island to pass Gwanjangmok. Nevertheless, many ships must have been being wrecked when their crews failed to spot the reefs hidden off the coast of Mado Island.

# The History of the Development of Korean Underwater Archaeology

Chapter 5

# The History of the Development of Korean Underwater Archaeology

In 1977, a total of 980 *wuzhuqian* coins(五銖錢) were found off the coast of Geomundo Island, Yeosu. A *wuzhuqian* is a Chinese coin that was first issued in the Han Dynasty and remained in circulation until the Sui Dynasty. These coins were assumed to be from a shipwreck, since wooden materials found with them appeared to be the remains of a hull. If that is the case, then what is the meaning of this large quantity of Chinese coins found in Geomundo Island in Korea? In fact, they constitute positive evidence that the West and South Seas of Korea were places of vigorous exchange between Korea and China.

Korea, as a country surrounded by water on three sides, has

actively engaged in trace and exchange with neighboring countries by sea routes since ancient times. Notably, the west and south coasts of Korea were the living spaces of our ancestors and important sea routes for connecting Korea with neighboring countries. As with the Mediterranean Sea which connects three continents, Asia, Europe and Africa, new cultural elements and goods were actively exchanged in the west and south of Korea as numerous ships came and went across these seas. Sometimes, these seas became the scene of major battles that determined a country's fate.

## The West and South Seas in Korea, the Main Field of Korean Underwater Archaeology

Marine exchange in the seas surrounding the Korean peninsula was conducted by using several seaways, notably the north and south routes, which connected Korea with China and Japan. The north route was divided into two passages; one along the north coast to the Shandong peninsula via Liaodong, the other across the West Sea to the Shandong Peninsula. The former was the route by which the Han Dynasty attacked Gojoseon, and by which the expeditionary forces of the Sui and Tang Dynasties invaded Goguryeo. Baekje and Silla used the latter route to dispatch envoys to China, since they were unable to communicate with China via the land routes. The troops of the Tang Dynasty led by Su Dingfang also used this route to invade Baekje.

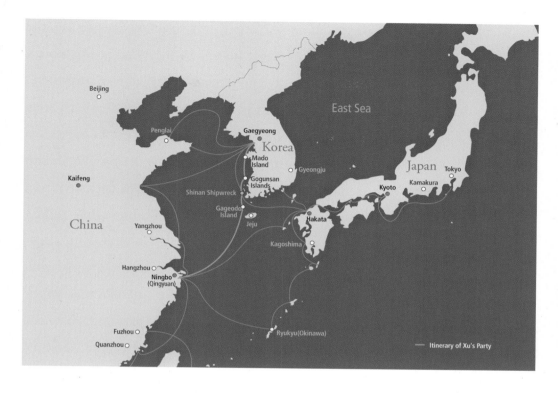

The south route, which connected Ningbo in China with Korea and Kyushu, was exploited as early as the north routes; but was more actively used from the Goryeo Period onward when shipbuilding and nautical skills were more developed, because it was rough route passing the East China Sea. Xu Jing, the author of *Xuanhe Fengshi Gaoli Tujing*(宣和奉使高麗圖經), a famous book describing the social and cultural customs of the Goryeo Dynasty, visited Goryeo via the south route, even though the north route across the West Sea was the fastest route between the Shandong peninsula and Gaegyeong in Goryeo. It appears that Xu's party took the south route due to the development of the Jin Dynasty in northern China. Xu Jing and his retinue set sail from Ningbo,

Network of Sea Routes of East Asia and the Itinerary of Xu's Party crossed the East China Sea, and finally reached Gaegyeong, the capital of Goryeo, via several islands in the West Sea in Korea, including Gageodo Island, the Gogunsando Islands, and Mado Island. This route was more frequently used in the Southern Song Dynasty Period when the Song Dynasty moved its capital to Hangzhou following an invasion by the Jin Dynasty. The Shinan Shipwreck, a merchant ship of the Yuan Dynasty, departed from Ningbo but was wrecked in the waters off Shinan while sailing toward Japan, its final destination.

In addition, the discovery of obsidian tools made of raw materials quarried in Japan, and Jomon pottery at shell midden sites on the west and south coast in Korea clearly attests to exchanges between the Korean peninsula and Kyushu in Japan during the Neolithic Period. The distance between the southern region of the Korean peninsula and Kyushu is relatively short, and Tsushima Island is located between the two regions.

Therefore, this route was actively used from as early as the prehistoric era and right through the Three Kingdoms and Goryeo Periods to the Joseon Period. In particular, the *Imjin Waeran* broke out when Japanese troops invaded Joseon in 1592 by crossing this route; and the West and South Seas of Korea became the scene of numerous naval battles between the navies of Joseon and Japan. Therefore, these seas were at the center of the marine exchange route of East Asia, and provided a space by which Korea could "network" with neighboring countries.

## Marine Environment of the West and South Seas of Korea

In the past, the maritime environment greatly influenced navigation because ships were dependent on sea and tidal currents and the wind for movement. In the Korean peninsula, the wind direction periodically changes from northwest in winter to southwest or southeast in summer, which meant that ships had to sail downwind to cross the wide sea. Xu's party departed on May 26, and arrived at Gageodo Island on June 2, crossing the East China Sea on a southwesterly wind. They arrived at Gaegyeong, the final destination, on June 12, by sailing northward along the coast of the West Sea. This was quite a short journey of less than twenty days.

During the Goryeo and Joseon Periods, many cargo vessels carrying grain collected from various parts of country sailed along

Celadon Cupstand Recovered from the Sea of Myeongnyangdae-cheop-ro

the west and south coastline toward Gaegyeong and Hanyang. As these vessels shipped grain collected as a tax for governing the state, they usually sailed between February and March when relatively weak winds prevailed. Despite the cautious voyage, there were many accidents in the West and South Seas due to strong tidal currents and topographical causes.

More than 3,000 islands are distributed in these seas which have large tidal ranges. Therefore, very strong tidal currents run between the islands, sometimes creating eddies. Even today, these factors present obstacles to safe navigation. Moreover, rocks hidden beneath the surface of the water were a common cause of shipwreck.

The sinking of a ship was of course an unfortunate accident and a disaster of the people on board. However, sunken ships represent a significant and invaluable source of information on the socio-cultural aspects of ancient societies. In particular, mud deposited on the seabed of these seas conserves hulls and objects loaded on the wrecked ship by protecting them from the decomposing effect of exposure to air or water. Although mud and silt cause low visibility and thus pose a considerable obstacle to underwater investigations, objects buried under them retain their original form. For this reason, we are able to observe the condition of shipwrecks at the time of their sinking. In this regard, one may say that Korean underwater archaeology has developed on the basis of mud deposited on the seabed.

## In Search of Geobukseon(Turtle Ship), the Dream of Korea's Underwater Archaeologists

Even before the field of underwater archaeology was introduced in Korea, the first investigation of underwater cultural heritage to use underwater exploration equipment(such as a side-scan sonar) was conducted at Chilcheonryang in Geojedo Island in July 1973. The purpose of this investigation was to locate a *geobukseon*(turtle ship), the armored battleship of the Joseon Navy that was used to devastating effect in the *Imjin Waeran*. With the assistance of

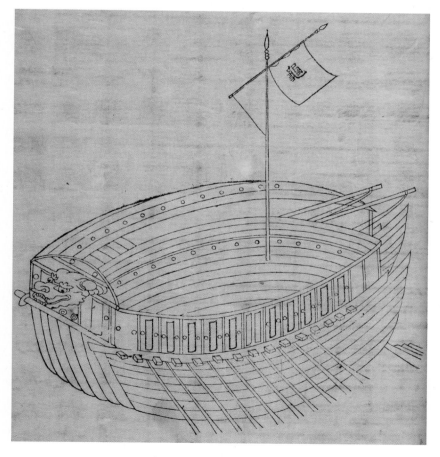

Illustration of a *Geobukseon* in *Gwonsudoseol* (卷首圖說), the Yi *Chungmugong Jeonseo*(李忠武公全書)

the Republic of Korea Navy and the Geological Survey of Korea (present-day Korean Institute of Geoscience and Mineral Resources), the Cultural Properties Administration(present-day Cultural Heritage Administration) carried out an investigation by mobilizing divers and using equipment, but no *geobukseon* was found in the investigated area. In 1978, the investigation team which conducted the underwater excavation of the Shinan Shipwreck reported that they had found a hull assumed to be a *geobukseon* off the coast of Dangpo; but divers eventually identified it as the wreck of a sunken fishing boat.

The attempt to find a *geobukseon* has continued uninterrupted. The Artifact Excavation Institution for the Naval Battles of Admiral Yi Sun-Sin(Posthumous title: *Chungmugong*), which was established by the Republic of Korea Navy in 1989, conducted a series of investigations at the sites of his naval battle during the Imjin Waeran, such as Chilcheonryang in Geoje, Hansando Island in Tongyeong, and Noryang in Namhae. In 1992, the institute announced the discovery of a *byeolhwangjachontong*, a type of cannon used on *geobukseon*. However, prosecutors revealed that it was an imitation. Captain Hwang, the head of the institute, disguised a replica of the cannon he had purchased at an antique shop as an excavated relic by dropping it into the waters off Hansando Island. This was a shocking affair for Korean academic circles.

A few years ago, Gyeongsangnam-do Provincial Office conducted a detailed investigation lasting from July 2008 to April 2009 of the waters of Chilcheonryang using a multi-beam echo sounder and a seismic profiler.

Although anomalous objects were detected in several spots, no remains of a *geobukseon* were identified. According to historical sources, the Korean Navy only had between three and five of these armored warships during the *Imjin Waeran*, so finding the remains of a hull or other artifacts from these ships is no easy task.

It will not be possible to satisfy people's curiosity about whether the *geobukseon* was really an armored warship or whether it had either two or three decks until the remains of a hull are discovered. The *geobukseon* has been recognized as a symbol of the pride of the Korean people and as the ship that saved the nation against the Japanese invasion; thus it has aroused considerable interest among the public as well as scholars. As such, if there is any possibility of finding one hidden under the mud on the seabed, an investigation to find a *geobukseon* could be the most important project and, ultimately, the most difficult challenge facing underwater archaeologists in Korea today.

## The Birth of Korean Underwater Archaeology in the 1970s-1980s: Korean Underwater Archaeology Begins with the Excavation of the Shinan Shipwreck

As explained in the previous chapters, Korean underwater archaeology began with the survey of the Shinan Shipwreck in 1976. Due to the great historical value of the numerous salvaged objects and hull structures, the project to investigate this shipwreck has been evaluated as one of the most important underwater excavation campaigns in the world. The first and second investigations, conducted from 26 October to 1 December 1976, revealed the hull as well as porcelain vessels and coins buried under the seafloor. After completing these two preliminary excavations, the institute conducted a series of full-scale excavations until 1984, and uncovered a total of 23,502 artifacts and rosewood objects, and 28 tons of coins.

Despite illegal looting and unfavorable underwater conditions, the excavation of the Shinan Shipwreck provided the necessary momentum for the birth of underwater archaeology in Korea, and enjoyed the full support of the Republic of Korean Navy, which provided divers and a rescue ship during the investigation campaigns. The navy divers spent a combined total of 3,474 hours under the sea.

In March 1983, when the underwater excavation of the Shinan Shipwreck was actively under way, the female divers of Jeju reported the discovery of several items including gold bracelets on the coast of Sinchang-ri, Jeju to the government office. The following month, the investigation team found two gold headdresses in the place where the female divers had found the other

**Monument to the Excavation of the Shinan Shipwreck**
Erected on Jeungdo Island, Shinan, Jeollanam-do Province, this monument records the procedure and significance of the underwater excavation of the Shinan Shipwreck, along with the names of the members of the excavation team, including the Cultural Properties Administration and the Republic of Korea Navy, from 1976 to 1984.

gold artifacts. An additional investigation of the Sinchang-ri Underwater Site conducted in 1996 revealed celadon vessels dating to the Southern Song Dynasty. These vessels are inscribed with Chinese characters such as *hebinyipan*(河濱遺范) and *jinyumantang*(金玉滿堂), a characteristic feature of celadon vessels fired at the Longquanyao Kiln in the Southern Song Period. No hull was identified at this site; but some fifty artifacts were recovered there.

From 1981 to 1987, short-term investigations were conducted along the coast of the Taean peninsula during the periods when the investigation of the Shinan Shipwreck was interrupted. In particular, about 100 celadon vessels including thirty-two inlaid celadon porcelains were found in the waters off Jukdo Island, Boryeong. Of these, a celadon bowl inlaid with the Chinese characters *gisa*(己巳 , 1269 or 1329 AD) provides important data for

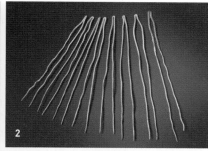

1 Gold Bracelet from Sinchang-ri Underwater Site
2 Gold Headdresses from Sinchang-ri Underwater Site
3 Celadon Bowl with Inlaid Chinese Characters, *Gisa*, from the Sea of Jukdo Island in Boryeong

Excavation
of the Wando
Shipwreck(Left),
Celadon Vessels
Salvaged from the
Wando Shipwreck
(Right)

the study of Goryeo celadon.

The excavation of the Wando Shipwreck was begun after two divers(fishermen) for clams on the coast of Eodu-ri, Joyakdo Island, Wando, reported their discovery of four celadon vessels to the district prosecutor's office. A preliminary survey of the area revealed that more than a thousand celadon vessels lay buried under mud. The investigation team excavated the area in the period between the end of the ninth excavation and the beginning of the tenth excavation of the Shinan Shipwreck.

The first excavation identified a dense cluster of artifacts on a rounded hillock measuring 50-60 meters in height and 10 meters in diameter; while the second excavation undertaken the following year exposed the hull, under which lay about 30,000 celadon vessels. This hull was the Wando Shipwreck.

Although parts of the bottom and side planks were excavated, this shipwreck, which was the sole Goryeo shipwreck excavated before Dalido shipwreck in 1995, has yielded much valuable data for research on the history of Goryeo ships. Most of the goods carried by this cargo vessel are low-quality celadon porcelains. It is assumed that this ship sank after encountering an unexpected accident while transporting celadon vessels.

## The Establishment of Foundation of Korean Underwater Archaeology in the 1990s: Shipwrecks Found on Mudflats

The excavation of the Shinan Shipwreck heralded a brilliant opening for Korean underwater archaeology; but, sadly, once the investigations of the Shinan and Wando Shipwrecks had been completed there were no further excavations for over ten years. During this period, academic investigation was impossible due to the absence of specialists, as the investigation team had relied

**Exposed Hull of Jindo Ship**
The ship was found in a waterway adjoining the salt field in Byeokpa Village

somewhat excessively on the SSU of the Republic of Korea navy until the late 1980s. However, Korean underwater archaeology did not stagnate entirely in the 1990s: The National Maritime Museum in Mokpo, opened in 1994, established a system of conservation treatment for ancient ships while conducting preservation work on the Shinan and Wando Shipwrecks. Moreover, the excavation campaigns of the two shipwrecks buried under mudflats not only extended the scope of Korean underwater archaeology but also lay the foundations for further investigations of wrecked ships.

In Korea shipwrecks have often been found on mudflats as well as on the seabed. Generally, the hulls of decommissioned ships and shipwrecks collapse and break apart over time. Therefore, parts of these ships are inevitably swept away by waves and currents; while other parts are eventually buried in mudflats. Many of the hulls buried in mudflats have been found by people collecting shells, crabs and octopuses. However, few objects remained in the hulls found in mudflats, since people were able to access and loot them easily.

*Baoshoukong* **Holes in the Jindo Shipwreck** This hole contained eight Chinese coins minted during the Northern Song Dynasty.

As with excavations conducted on land, implement such as shovels, trowels and brushes are the main tools used to excavate a hull buried in a mudflat. In 1991 and 1992, the investigation team first excavated a hull buried in a mudflat in Korea. This was the Jindo Shipwreck, which was built with large logs of camphor wood. This species of tree grows in Korea and Japan; but trees of the type used to build large ships such as the Jindo Shipwreck grow south of the Yangtze River. Also found in the hull were little holes called *baoshoukong*, into which coins or bronze mirrors were inserted during prayers for a safe voyage. As this ritual was practiced mainly in Fujian Province, some scholars have conjectured that this ship was built in China. However, few ships were built of logs in China in the thirteenth and fourteenth centuries; rather, a similar type of ship to the Jindo Shipwreck was built in Japan during this period, leading some scholars to argue that it was a Japanese ship. In particular, Japanese raiders frequently invaded Goryeo in this period. If this was a ship built in Japan, it may well have been a pirate(*wakou*) ship. In addition, it is not easy conserve structures made of camphor wood, because there are easily wrapped. The institute is still conducting conservation treatment on the hull of the Jindo shipwreck, which was salvaged over twenty years ago.

Three years later, the Dalido Shipwreck was excavated in the Jipeungol mudflat located northwest of Dalido Island in Mokpo. A local resident found the hull of the ship in 1989 while catching long-legged octopus. In 1994, another local resident from the same village unearthed a bronze spoon, two dishes, and large quantities of porcelain fragments, and reported his discovery to the local government office. A system and method of excavating the hull from the mudflat was established during the first excavation(survey) of this ship in the summer of 1995. First, in

order to prevent penetrating of water soaked in mudflat, ditches were dug around the hull; second, roads that could be moved by the investigators were made; third, a three-story scaffold was built for taking photos; and fourth, meshes were installed around the hull to prevent the loss of the vestiges of the hull and other artifacts.

Generally, when investigators excavate hulls in mudflats, they face severe time constraints as excavation work can only be conducted during low tide. The mudflat where the Dalido Shipwreck lay buried allowed only two hours of investigation work per day, and even then the investigators spent a lot of time bailing water out of the hull. After completing the packing of the hull for transportation, an unfortunate incident occurred as the hull was flooded when the high tide rose ahead of the expected time, forcing the investigators to cling on to the hull to prevent it from being carried away by the surging water. Fortunately, a crane arrived in time to lift it.

The remaining hull, which measures 10.5 meters in length and 2.72 meters in width, contained few artifacts. As this was the first shipwreck to be excavated since the Wando Shipwreck, it was difficult to determine its construction date solely by examining the hull structure and construction method. For these reasons, research on this shipwreck relied on scientific method; radiocarbon dating of samples collected from the hull indicated that the ship was built in the thirteenth-fourteenth century AD.

In October 1995, divers reported their discovery of about 120 inlaid celadon vessels while they were catching clams off the coast

Celadon Vessels with Inlaid Design Recovered from the Doripo Underwater Site in Muan

of Doripo, Muan, to the local government office. Immediately afterward, an excavation of the area where the vessels were found was begun, in which the Excavation Institution for the Naval Battles of Admiral Yi Sunsin also participated. The investigation team made an unsuccessful attempt to find the hull, which they assumed contained celadon vessels, using survey equipment of the Republic of Korea Navy. As with the previous investigations, navy divers surveyed the seabed. Nevertheless, three underwater investigations recovered some 638 celadon vessels, all but ten of which were inlaid celadon porcelains produced at Sadang-ri, Gangjin in the fourteenth century, and a polished stone dagger.

## Major Leap Forward of Korean Underwater Archaeology in the 2000s: Establishment of an Independent Investigation System

From 2000 onwards, Korean underwater archaeology made huge strides in both the qualitative and quantitative aspects. Henceforth, the investigation team was able to conduct annual underwater excavations without the assistance of the navy, a development that originated from the endeavors of the National Maritime Museum, which equipped itself with a side-scan sonar and a seismic profiler to lay the basis for underwater excavations, and conducted a diving training program to its staff with the aim of acquiring the capacity to conduct underwater investigations by itself. Although the museum began its independent investigations

by borrowing fishing boats, it was able to conduct more active and specialized investigations at Kkamakseom Island in Gochang(1999) and Sisando Island in Yeonggwang(2000).

Seven years after the underwater excavation at Doripo in Muan, in 2002, excavation of the Biando site in Gunsan began, after a fisherman reported his discovery of 243 celadon vessels while diving to find a lost dragnet for catching conches. The museum conducted a series of five underwater investigations in 2002-2003. Although the navy assisted the first investigation, the investigation team had to conduct the second investigation without its assistance due to the outbreak of the Battle of Yeonpyeong in the West Sea in 2002. Therefore, the museum staff themselves dived into the water to identify the distribution pattern of the artifacts and take photos of them.

This investigation was largely focused on recording artifacts that were scattered on the seabed. Although the hull of the ship was not found, the team uncovered two wooden objects that appeared to be oars, and about 2,900 celadon vessels. Most of the vessels found at this site were plain type celadon wares either with no decorative features or decorated with incised and carved designs. The reason for the discovery of many so celadon vessels off the coast of Biando Island is closely related with the Saemangeum Land Reclamation Project. As seawater repeatedly flowed in and out of the narrow gap between the seawalls built from Sinsido and Garyeokdo Islands, the strong tidal current running between the two structures swept away a mud layer deposited on the seabed at a depth of 6 meters. After completing the construction work on the seawall, the speed of the tidal current that runs through the site decreased. The results of a second resurvey of this site conducted in 2007 show that the site was re-buried under a mud layer about 1 meter deep.

In winter 2003, when the excavation of the Biando site was completed, the museum began a new underwater excavation campaign at Sipidonpado Island in Gunsan. In Korea, underwater excavations have been carried out every year without interruption since 2003.

In 2003, a diver reported his discovery of celadon vessels while catching butter clams to the local government office. In order to catch this species, divers usually shoot high-pressure water into the holes inhabited by them. On this occasion, the celadon vessel came up with the clams. However, at first the museum could not obtain accurate information about the location where the celadon vessels were found as the diver disappeared immediately after filing his report, doubtless because he was worried about being prosecuted for his illegal fishing activities. Fortunately, the museum staffs were able to communicate with him with the assistance of the coast guard, and eventually found out that more artifacts and parts of the hull remained at that place. The survey conducted in the area indicated by the fisherman revealed the Sipidongpado Shipwreck, which lay buried at a gradient of 15° to the left and measured 7 meters in length and 2.5 meters in width. The hull was found to contain neatly stacked Goryeo celadon vessels packed in wooden frames and bound with straw ropes, making it the second celadon freighter to be discovered in the Korean peninsula.

Of the coastal areas where underwater excavation have been conducted so far, the coast at Sipidongpado Island was the best place due to its good visibility(about 4 meters) and the moderate velocity of the tidal currents. When the investigators removed the sediment, water containing mud naturally flowed. This was the best environment for conducting an underwater excavation, and cannot be compared with the marine environment at Biando Island, which is characterized by low visibility and strong tidal currents. Therefore, the investigators were able to attempt a

Sipidongpado Shipwreck(Left), Investigator Conducting Measurement Survey(Right)

measurement survey as well as underwater an photography shoot. The excavation of this shipwreck uncovered about 8,100 celadon vessels produced at Sindeok-ri in Haenam in the twelfth century, as well as objects used by the crew, such as iron caldrons, bronze spoons, and stone plates(hearths).

Along with the underwater excavations, excavations of the mud-flats were also carried out. In 1995, ten years after the excavation of the Dalido site, a hull was discovered on a mudflat in Anjwado Island, Shinan. The person who reported the discovery of seven fragments of the celadon vessels to the government office also stated that a hull had been gradually exposed by erosion of the mudflat about three years previously. The excavation of the Anjwa

Excavation of the Anjwa Shipwreck

Shipwreck was conducted over a period of forty days in summer 2005. As well two celadon cups and three celadon dishes produced at Sadang-ri in Gangjin in the fourteenth century, the hull also yielded a number of stoneware jars, whetstones, and wooden logs. In Korea, excavated shipwrecks are often found to contain many wooden logs that were laid on the bottom or leaned against the wall of the hull to prevent water logging of the cargo if water entered the hull. When such wooden logs were first identified at the Anjwa Shipwreck, the investigators, unaware of their true purpose, initially mistook them for firewood.

In 2005, a slightly unusual excavation was conducted in Won-sando Island, leading to the discovery of high-quality celadon fragments spread across a wide mudflat that was only exposed for 4-5 days during the spring tide. Therefore, the excavation team removed the silt using shovels and water jets at the spring tide, and conducted an aquanautic investigation while the mudflat was

Shards of Celadon
Vessels Scattered
on the Mudflat at
Wonsando Island

covered by seawater.

In addition to dishes, various types of celadon porcelains including incense burners, pillows, chairs, and water droppers were uncovered at this site. One curious fact is that all of the vessels were broken into pieces except for one dish. In many cases in Korea, unbroken celadon vessels have been found by underwater excavations. Therefore the reason for the breakage at this site has not yet been elucidated. The fragments collected from the mudflat of Wonsando Island belonged to Goryeo celadon vessels of the highest quality, like those made for members of the royal family. As such, it is assumed that these goods were produced in Gangjin in the thirteenth century and formed part of the cargo of a ship bound for Gaegyeong that sank in this area.

The Daebudo Shipwreck was discovered in the mudflat at Daebudo Island, Ansan in 2006. Parts of the hull had sunk deep into the sandy flat. This shipwreck displays a similar hull structure to other Goryeo shipwrecks found in Korea.

## The Progress of Korean Underwater Archaeology

In recent years, Korean underwater archaeology has succeeded in establishing a firm foothold for major growth in the future. An official department for underwater excavation was established at the National Maritime Museum in March 2007; and, that same month, the Sea Muse, Korea's first underwater exploration vessel, input to survey the Geumhoho Lake in Haenam. Launched in November 2006, the Sea Muse has been conducting surveys aimed at detecting underwater cultural heritages lying buried under the bed of Korean seas. After taking on board the surveying and diving equipment, there is little space left for the investigators' relaxation. However, the Sea Muse has made a highly significant

Locations of the Yamido and Biando Underwater Sites

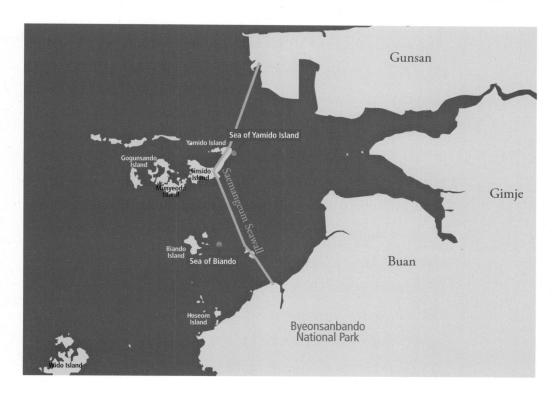

contribution to the development of Korean underwater archaeology thanks to its monumental discoveries of Mado Shipwreck Nos. 1, 3 and 4, and the Yeongheungdo Shipwreck.

As if in response to these developments, the discovery of a celadon dish caught up in a fisherman's trap along with a webfoot octopus off the coast of Daeseom Island in Taean in May 2007 opened up a new chapter in the history of Korean underwater archaeology. The resultant survey was undertaken due to the flurry of newspaper articles published about this story. The survey revealed that numerous celadon vessels were scattered across the seabed at a depth of 12 meters. In order to prevent illegal looting, the Cultural Heritage Administration designated this area as a cultural heritage protection zone and prohibited diving, since the mass media had already announced the discovery of celadon vessels in this area. The full-scale excavation conducted from July produced great results, including the discovering of about 25,000 celadon porcelains and the hull of the Taean Shipwreck, a celadon cargo vessel of the Goryeo Dynasty.

Above all, public recognition of the importance of the underwater cultural heritage was the most significant achievement of this excavation, particularly as public interest in underwater cultural heritage and excavation had gradually petered out after the excavation of the Shinan Shipwreck. Under these circumstances, the discovery of numerous Goryeo celadon porcelains in the Taean Shipwreck reawakened public attention.

The underwater excavation of the Yamido site in Gunsan was another important achievement of Korean underwater archaeology during this period. This site was initially brought to light by the arrest of looters. Two excavations of this site in 2006 and 2007 revealed myriad low-quality celadon porcelains fired in the twelfth century.

**Improved Scuba Gear**
Investigators on board can monitor the underwater situation and communicate with divers.

As with the discovery of the Biando site, the underwater excavation of the Yamido site is closely related to the Saemangeum Land Reclamation Project. When construction of the embankment began, the speed of nearby tidal currents accelerated, and many artifacts were exposed by erosion of the seafloor. Upon completion of the embankment, the velocity of the tidal currents slowed, and the site was buried under mud deposited on the seabed. After the excavation of the Taean Shipwreck, a third excavation of the site was conducted in 2008, during which time the underwater survey equipment was greatly improved.

Two new barges were built for the specific purpose of underwater surveys. The barge used previously was a small boat(3×4 meters) that provided a poor environment for surveys. The investigators suffered from engine noise and the exhaust of the underwater air-supply device. However, the new barges(14×16 meters) enabled the investigators to conduct various works, such as removing silt, diving, and assembling artifacts. The equipment for removing

3×4 meters
Barge(Left),
14×16 meters
Barge(Right)

silt was also improved and optimized for Korea's marine environment. Prior to this excavation, an air lift was the main item of equipment for removing silt; however, as the hose for removing silt stood vertically in the water, it was buffeted about by tidal currents, and had difficulty thoroughly removing silt in shallow water, among other problems. The use of a vacuum pump saw an improvement on the weaknesses of the air lift pump, as its hose can be laid horizontally on the bottom of the seabed, thus preventing it from being moved by tidal currents. Moreover, the investigators were able to conduct a more detailed excavation without having to worry about controlling its buoyancy.

The underwater excavation techniques accumulated during the excavation of the Taean Shipwreck and the Yamido Island sites provided the impetus for the underwater excavation of Mado Shipwreck Nos. 1, 2 and 3 off the coast of Mado Island from 2009. Unlike other excavated Goryeo shipwrecks, which were celadon cargo vessels, these ships contained diverse cargos including grains and salted fermented seafood, and, perhaps more importantly, wooden tablets and cargo tags recording the identities of the senders and receivers of the cargos. The discovery of items providing information on social aspects of the Goryeo Period served as the momentum for further academic development of Korean underwater archaeology.

## The Current Status of Underwater Archaeology in Korea

Another great leap forward in the field of Korean underwater archaeology occurred when the Nurian, a newly constructed underwater exploration ship, was launched in 2013. This 290 ton ship is designed to enable about twenty investigators to conduct underwater surveys for twenty days, and a maximum of eight investiga-

The Nurian(Right), The Sea Muse(Left)

tors to dive at any one time. Furthermore, this ship carries various items of advanced underwater excavation equipment including devices for removing silt, lifts for salvaging artifacts and hulls, artifact storage facilities, and an on-deck decompression chamber.

The ship was first used in the excavation of the Yeongheungdo Shipwreck in Incheon. The survey of this site, which was undertaken after the reporting of four celadon porcelains in 2010, discovered large quantities of celadon vessels. A sunken hull containing stoneware vessels and iron caldrons had been found in the first excavation conducted back in 2002. However, it was difficult to carry out the excavation using the Sea Muse and wooden barges because the site is located in an area characterized by strong waves, winds and tidal currents. Thus the investigation team had to wait for the launch of the Nurian in order to carry out a full-scale excavation in the second investigation in 2013.

The excavation of the Yeongheungdo Shipwreck revealed three large hull fragments held under a dozen of heavy iron caldrons; however, it seems that the other parts of the hull were either scattered or carried far away by the strong tidal currents. The rust on the iron caldrons had caused them to become entangled with stoneware jars from the hull. Therefore, the investigators were able to collect further artifacts

An Investigator Removing Iron Rust from the Yeongheungdo Shipwreck

simply by removing the rust from the caldrons.

Initially, it was assumed that this ship was a Goryeo vessel as numerous Goryeo celadon porcelains lay scattered around the hull. However, the results of an analysis of the absolute dates indicate that the ship was built in the eighth century during the Unified Silla Period. Moreover, the hull contained no Goryeo celadon, yielding instead stoneware vessels of shapes similar to those produced in the Unified Silla Period. Therefore, it is the earliest extant traditional Korean ship salvaged by an underwater investigation to date.

The Sea of Myeongnyangdaecheop-ro in Jindo is the second site at which the Nurian played an active role. This site is located 4.3 kilometers southeast of the Uldolmok Strait where the Battle of Myeongnyang took place during the *Imjin Waeran*. Annual excavations conducted from 2012 to 2014 revealed some important artifacts including plain earthenware from the Proto-Three Kingdoms Period, high-quality Goryeo celadon wares, notably, a qilin-shaped incense burner, and three *sososeungjachongtong*(小小勝字銃筒), a type of cannon used by the Korean navy during the *Imjin Waeran*. One of these cannons is incised with the Chinese characters <萬曆戊子/四月日左營/造小小勝字/重三斤九/兩/匠尹德永>, which means "A cannon made at the Left Jeolla Naval Base in April 1588; weight: three *geun* nine *nyang*; product of the craftsman Yun Deokyeong." Cannons such as these were personal arms in the mid-Joseon Period. However, although such weapons as *sungja, chaseungja, byeolseungja,* and *soseungja* are all recorded

A *Sososeungja-chongtong* Cannon Recovered from the Sea of *Myeongnyangdae-cheop-ro* Site(57.8 centimeters in length)(Left), Clay, Paper and Gunpowder Found in the *Sososeung-jachongtong* Cannons(Right)

in historical sources; there is no record of the *sososeungja* cannon. In fact, this is the first *sososeungja* ever discovered. The clay, paper, and gunpowder found in the barrels of these three cannons unequivocally demonstrate that they fell into the water during a battle against the enemy fleet or a naval exercise.

In addition, an annual underwater excavation has been conducted off the coast of Mado Island, the representative underwater site in Korea; and the Seohae Research Institute of Maritime Cultural Heritage is being built at Sinjindo Island in Taean. Underwater excavation off the coast of Mado in 2015 revealed the hull of Mado Shipwreck No. 4. As the first Joseon cargo vessel ever found, it has provided the impetus for extending the scope of Korean underwater archaeology.

Moreover, Daebudo Shipwreck No. 2, the other Goryeo Shipwreck covered by the mudflat at Daebudo Island, was excavated. The hull of this ship, which was discovered by a local resident while fishing for long-legged octopus, exhibits a different structure from other Goryeo ships, being somewhat smaller and narrower. Unlike other shipwrecks found in the mudflat, this ship also has a

space that is assumed to be the crew's living space, judging by the fact that it contained four bronze spoons, celadon dishes, bronze vessels, and stoneware vessels for storing water and foods.

During the dismantling work, seeds and flesh of dried persimmons were found perfectly intact in the lower part of the hull, causing the investigators to exclaim aloud as they caught the scent of this ancient fruit. Harvested many hundreds of years ago in the Goryeo Period, the persimmons were preserved by the marine environment. With the exception of Wando Shipwreck, all of the underwater surveys and excavations have been carried out in the West Sea, which suggests that many marine accidents occurred there. Considering that the South Sea was traversed by important coastal routes, and was a ferocious battlefield in the *Imjin Waeran*, it is possible that myriad materials are distributed around this seafloor. Therefore,

Excavation of
Mado Shipwreck
No. 4

Excavation of
Daebudo
Shipwreck No. 2

it is to be hoped that further discoveries at new sites in the South Sea will serve as the catalyst for continuous development of Korean underwater archaeology.

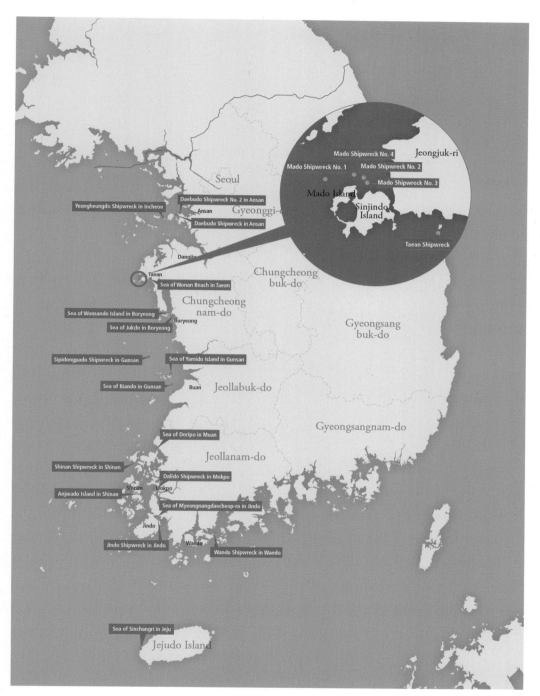

Map of the Underwater Sites in Korea

# ● History of Underwater Excavation of Korea ●

| No | Year | Site | Excavation research institution | Feature of Cultural Heritage |
|---|---|---|---|---|
| 1 | 1976~1984 | Shinan Shipwreck in Shinan | Cultural Properties Administration & Republic of Korea Navy | Excavation of merchant ship of the Yuan Dynasty<br>The first underwater excavation of Korea |
| 2 | 1980, 1983, 1996 | Sea of Sinchang-ri in Jeju | Cultural Properties Administration /Jeju national university Museum | Discovery of golden accessories and celadon vessels of the Song Dynasty |
| 3 | 1981~1987 | Sea of Taean Peninsula (Jukdo in Boryeong) | Cultural Properties Administration, & Republic of Korea Navy | Discovery of celadon and white procelain including celadon bowl with inlaid Chinese character 'gisa(己巳)' |
| 4 | 1983~1984 | Wando Shipwreck in Wando | Cultural Properties Administration | Excavation a Gorye celadon cargo ship of 12th century<br>The first discovery of Korean traditional vessel |
| 5 | 1991~1992 | Jindo Shipwreck in Jindo | Mokpo Conservation Institute for Maritime Archaeological finds | Excavation of a large dugout of 13-14th centuries |
| 6 | 1995 | Dalido Shipwreck in Mokpo | National Maritime Museum | Excavation of a Goryeo vessel of 13-14th centuries |
| 7 | 1995~1996 | Sea of Doripo in Muan | National Maritime Museum & Republic of Korea Navy | Discovery of 638 celadon vessels with inlaid design of the Goryeo Dynasty |
| 8 | 2002~2003 | Sea of Biando in Gunsan | National Maritime Museum & Republic of Korea Navy | Discovery of about 2,900 celadon vessels of the Goryeo Dynasty |
| 9 | 2003~2004 | Sipidongpado Shipwreck in Gunsan | National Maritime Museum | Excavation of a Goryeo celadon cargo ship of 12th century |
| 10 | 2004~2005 | Sea of Wonsando Island in Boryeong | National Maritime Museum | Discovery of fragments of high-quality celadon on mud flat |
| 11 | 2005 | Anjwa Shipwreck in Shinan | National Maritime Museum | Excavation of a Goryeo ship of 14th century |
| 12 | 2006~2009 | Sea of Yamido Island in Gunsan | National Maritime Museum | Discovery of 4,547 Goryeo celadon vessels |
| 13 | 2006 | Daebudo Shipwreck in Ansan | National Maritime Museum | Excavation of a Goryeo ship of 12-13th centuries |

| # | Year | Site | Institution | Details |
|---|------|------|-------------|---------|
| 14 | 2007~2008 | Taean Shipwreck in Taean | National Maritime Museum | Excavation of a Goryeo celadon cargo ship of 12th century<br>The first discovery of wooden tablets of the Goryeo Dynasty |
| 15 | 2008~2010 | Sea of Mado & Mado Shipwreck No. 1 in Taean | National Research Institute of Maritime Cultural Heritage | The first Excavation of a grain carrier of the Goryeo Dynasty |
| 16 | 2009~2010 | Sea of Mado & Mado Shipwreck No. 1 in Taean | National Research Institute of Maritime Cultural Heritage | Excavation of a grain carrier of the Goryeo Dynasty<br>Discovery of prunus vases with wooden tablets |
| 17 | 2010 | Sea of Wonan Beach in Taean | National Research Institute of Maritime Cultural Heritage | Discovery of Goryeo celadon vessels |
| 18 | 2011 | Mado Shipwreck No. 3 | National Research Institute of Maritime Cultural Heritage | Excavation of a Goryeo cargo ship of 13th century |
| 19 | 2011~2012 | Sea of Mado in Taean | National Research Institute of Maritime Cultural Heritage | Discovery of Goryeo celadon vessels, etc. |
| 20 | 2010, 2012~2013 | Yeongheungdo Shipwreck in Incheon | National Research Institute of Maritime Cultural Heritage | The First Excavation of a ship of the Unified Silla Period |
| 21 | 2012~2014 | Sea of Myeongnangdaecheop-ro in Jindo | National Research Institute of Maritime Cultural Heritage | Discovery of three 'sososeungja' cannons used by Joseon navy during Imjin waeran |
| 22 | 2014 | Sea of Mado in Taean | National Research Institute of Maritime Cultural Heritage | Discovery of batches of white porcelains, and Mado Shipwreck No. 4 |
| 23 | 2015 | Mado Shipwreck No. 4 | National Research Institute of Maritime Cultural Heritage | The first excavation of a government-run tax carrier of the Joseon Dynasty |
| 24 | 2015 | Daebudo Shipwreck No. 2 in Ansan | National Research Institute of Maritime Cultural Heritage | Excavation of a Goryeo vessel of 12-13th centuries |
| 25 | 2016 | Sea of Myeongnangdaecheop-ro in Jindo | National Research Institute of Maritime Cultural Heritage | Discovery of Goryeo celadon vessels, etc. |

## Part 2

# Time Capsules in the Sea,
## the Search for Lost History

# The History of Traditional Korean Ships Revealed by Shipwrecks on the Seabed

# The History of Traditional Korean Ships Revealed by Shipwrecks on the Seabed

Before the invention of the aircraft, the ship was the most convenient and efficient means of transportation in human history. In particular, Korea, which is surrounded by water on three sides, engaged in trade and exchange with neighboring cultures from the Gojoseon to the Three Kingdoms Period by exploiting various sea routes. Goryeo appears to have engaged actively in maritime activities as it was called the 'Maritime Kingdom.' Moreover, Korea could defend itself against invasion by Japanese raiders by using warships, such as the *panokseon*(board-roofed ship) and the *geobukseon*(turtle ship), during the Joseon Period. In the decades after its liberation from Japanese occupation in 1945, Korea became a global leader of the shipbuilding industry on the basis of the striking development of shipbuilding engineering.

The history of Korean ships originated in the prehistoric age. In the beginning, people crossed rivers simply by drifting across them on wooden logs, and then expanded their living space along riversides and coasts by building simple boats composed of wooden logs. Over time, boats became larger and their structure more complex in order to resist waves and sail on the sea. This type of vessel is a ship rather than a boat. Nowadays, ships are used extensively to transport large quantities of people and goods at one time as well as for fishing activities.

Nevertheless, maritime accidents increased as shipping activities became ever more extensive. In spite of desperate efforts, many ships continued to be swept away by rough waves and run

The raft is the most basic type of boat design, and is characterized by the absence of a hull. Rafts were used extensively in pre-modern Korea.

aground, often resulting in shipwrecks. Indeed, numerous shipwrecks have been identified on the seabed and mudflats around Korea. Of fourteen uncovered shipwrecks, twelve(excluding the Jindo Shipwreck, a dugout boat, and the Shinan Shipwreck, a merchant vessel of the Yuan Dynasty) are traditional Korean ships.

## The Structure of 'Hanseon,' the Traditional Korean Ship

The Korean traditional ship, or *hanseon*(韓船), developed in accordance with the maritime environment of the Korean peninsula. Its structure is clearly distinguishable from ships in China and Japan as well as from western ships. Sadly, the *hanseon* disappeared as a result of improvements made to fishing craft during the Japanese occupation and after Korea's liberation. Nevertheless, twelve shipwrecks uncovered by water excavations and found in mudflats clearly show the main characteristics of the *hanseon* and its development pattern.

Only the structures below the deck remained of the *hanseon* ships uncovered by underwater excavations. Their deck and on-deck structures were lost, since it took a certain period of time to cover mud on shipwreck made of wood, and the exposed hulls were easily swept away

**Gageodo Ship (Reconstruction)** This ship was used for fishing anchovies at Gageodo Island in Shinan from the sixteenth century onward.

**Mado Shipwreck No. 3 after Investigation**
The ship's deck was swept. The photo shows the bottom planks, side planks, bow planks and *Garyong* supports.

by tidal currents among other causes. Structures under the deck consist of external structures including bottom planks, side planks, bows, sterns, and internal structures such as *garyong*(beams) and *meonge*(yoke-shaped supports).

The flat-bottomed hull is the main characteristic of Korean traditional ships. A V-shaped-bottomed ship that meets little water resistance is faster than a flat-bottomed ship. In general, the West built V-shaped bottomed ships; while China used both flat-bottomed and V-shaped-bottomed ships.

The reason why the traditional Korean ship has flat-bottomed hull is closely related to the maritime environment of Korea. Due to the large tidal range in the West and South Seas in Korea, the bottom of the hull put on the seafloor during the ebb tide. The Korean traditional ship with its flat bottom could rest safely on the floor during this time. This clearly shows the wisdom of the

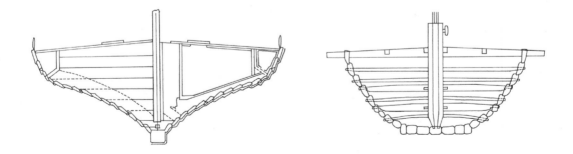

(From left) Cross-section of the Shinan Ship(V-shaped Bottom) and Mado Shipwreck No. 1(Flat Bottom)

ancestors of the Koreans.

The method of connecting bottom planks and garboard strakes illustrates the pattern of development of Goryeo shipbuilding technology. Rabbets, which were cut into the four sides of wooden logs, were directly connected with garboard strakes. The strakes in the side plank were horizontally connected by the half-lab jointing method, and were vertically connected by grooved clinkers, i.e. *pisak*(a mortise and tenon joint with a peg).

*Garyong*, the beams supporting the side planks, are a characteristic feature of Korean traditional ships. Chinese junks had bulkheads called *gebi*(隔壁) that supported the side flank so as to resist water pressure and prevent water flooding into one bulkhead from flowing into another bulkhead. However, Korean traditional ships did not have bulkheads; and each part of a ship was only joined by wooden nails. These unique structures are closely related to the *gaesak*(改槊) process.

*Gaesak* is the process of overhauling a Korean traditional ship. The

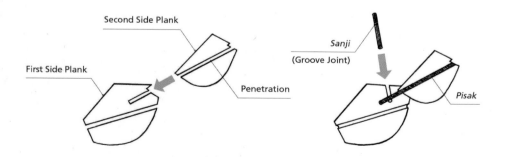

Cross-section of the Half-lab Jointing Method of Mado Shipwreck No. 1

hull of a ship that had sailed for a given period was disassembled in order to replace decayed structures and joints with new ones. It is not easy to pull out corroded iron joints, but shipbuilders could easily replace wooden joints with new ones. Compared with ship fitted with bulkheads, ships installed *with garyong* supports could be disassembled and reassembled far more easily.

*The Gyeonggukdaejeon*(經國大典), a complete code of law of the Joseon Dynasty, stipulated that the term of service of government-run ships, such as tax carriers, should be twenty years, and that such ships should be overhauled in the eighth year and fourteenth years after their construction.

The *hanseon* was built in consideration of Korea's maritime environment, and was thus characterized by a flat bottom, wooden joints, and the absence of bulkheads.

**Bulkheads of the Shinan Shipwreck**
Unlike Korean ships, the Shinan Shipwreck built in China had seven bulkheads.

# ● Structure of Traditional Korean Ship ●

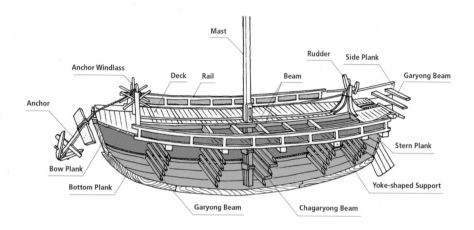

## Bow Plank(Imulbiu)

After connecting several vertically erected wooden planks with wooden tenons, and then inserting them into a V-shaped grooves on the bottom planks.

Bow Structure of Mado Shipwreck No. 3(Left) and Daebudo Shipwreck No. 2(Center), Connection between Bow Plank and Bottom Strakes in Daebudo Shipwreck No. 2(Right)

## Stern Plank(Gomulbiu)

After grooving both side planks and bottom planks, and inserting planks at the horizontal level. Stern planks are thinner than bow planks.

Stern Stakes of Daebudo Shipwreck No. 2 (After Disassembling Work)(Left), Groove Inserting Stern Plank(Right)

## Anchor(*Dat*)

An anchor is a device used to connect a vessel to the bed of a body of water to prevent it from drifting due to winds or currents. A wooden anchor is too light by itself to hook into the seabed, so it attached with heavy stones. Many anchor stones have been discovered, but few wooden anchors have been found as they are easily damaged or decomposed in the underwater environment.

Illustration and a Photo of an Anchor(Left) and a Stone Found in the Sea of Mado(Right)

## Rudder(*Key or Ta*)

A rudder is a part of the steering apparatus of a boat or ship that is fastened outside the hull. Few traditional Korean rudders have been found.

Rudder of Mado Shipwreck No. 2

## Bottom Plank(*Jeopan*)

The planks on the bottom of the hull are the thickest. Generally, the bottom consists of odd numbers of rows of planks, i.e. three rows in the Sipidonpado, Dalido and Anjwa Shipwrecks, five rows in the Wando Shipwreck and Mado Shipwreck No. 3, and seven rows in Mado Shipwreck Nos. 1 and 2. Only Daebudo Shipwreck No. 2 has a bottom strake consisting of even numbers of rows(four). The *hanseon* is characterized by a flat bottom strake connecting rows of planks with a *jangsak*, a long rectangular wooden tenon.

Bottom planks of the Wando Shipwreck(Left) and Daebudo Shipwreck No. 2(Center) and an Illustration of the Jointing Method for Bottom Planks(Right)

## Side Plank(*Oepan*)

Both the side strakes of the hull are piled up with wooden planks. The number of levels depends on the size of the hull. Mado Shipwreck No. 3 retains ten levels on the left side and nine on the right side, while Mado Shipwreck No. 4 has four levels on the left side and eleven on the right side. It seems that the eleventh plank on the right side represents the uppermost level.

Side Planks of the Dalido Shipwreck(Left) and Daebudo Shipwreck No. 2(Right)

## Anchor Windlass(*Horong*)

An anchor windlass is a device that restrains and manipulates the anchor chain. It is installed on deck. A few traditional Korean windlasses have been identified in underwater surveys. Ropes wound around a windlass have been found in the Sea around Mado Island and at Daebudo Shipwreck No. 2. A windlass support with grooves for spinning windlass was identified in the Sipidongpado Shipwreck.

Windlass in the Sea around Mado Island(Left), Windlass from Daebudo Shipwreck No. 2(Center), Windlass Support from the Sipidongpado Shipwreck(Right)

## Yoke-shaped Support(*Meonge*)

The yoke-shaped support is the pillar of the hull. It is placed in grooves on the uppermost planks to port and starboard to withstand water pressure. No yoke-shaped support has been found in an underwater survey in Korea.

## Beam(*Garyong*)

The beam's function is the same as the yoke-shaped support. A *garyong* was installed under the yoke-shaped support by inserting it into the hole of the planks on the side strakes. A yoke-shaped beam(*chagaryong*) is thinner than a yoke-shaped support and thicker than a *garyong*. It is placed in grooves in planks. The *dangappul*, a wooden structure supporting the mast, is installed in the yoke-shaped beam.

Beam and Yoke-shaped Beam from Daebudo Shipwreck No. 2(Left) *Dangappul* from the Dalido Shipwreck(Right)

## Mast(*Dotdae*)

The mast of a sailing vessel is a tall spar, or an arrangement of spars, erected more or less vertically on the center-line of a ship or boat. Supports are installed on its left and right sides respectively. A mast is inserted into the hole in the central row of the bottom strake.

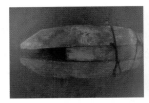 

Mast(Left) and Mast Hole(Right) from Mado Shipwreck No. 3

## The Development of Korean Traditional Ships

The dugout canoe is the proto-type of Korean traditional ships. The excavation of the Bibong-ri site in Changnyeong yielded two dugout boats built in around 8000 BC and a paddle dating to 7000 BC, the Neolithic Age. This site is now located in an inland area, but back then it was in a brackish water zone. These canoes exhibit a simplistic structure akin to a raft, and bear traces of burning to assist the hollowing out of logs at several points on their surface. A dugout boat is called a '*masangi*' or '*maesangi*' in Korean.

It is difficult to ascertain with any exactitude the development and transition pattern of Korean traditional ships from the Neolithic Age to the Three Kingdoms Period, because no boats or ships built in these periods have been found except for Bibong-ri Dugout Nos. 1 and 2. Nevertheless, the scenes of whale hunting at the Bangudae Petroglyphs site demonstrate that prehistoric Koreans conducted maritime activities. The form of the vessels built in the Three Kingdoms Period can be inferred from the boat-shaped potteries yielded from ancient tombs from that era. A boat-shaped pottery uncovered from the Geumryeongchong Tomb

**Paddle Discovered at the Bibong-ri Site(Upper)**
The paddle consists of a shaft and a blade.
**Bibong-ri Boat No. 1(Lower)**
The remaining structure measures 310 centimeters long, 62 centimeters wide, and 2-5 centimeters thick.

in Gyeongju is a representative example, as it displays a dugout with a raised bow and a stern. A dugout has two levels of side planks. A structure connecting both side planks is also described. This figure shows the pattern of development of dugouts.

Boat-shaped Pottery
Recovered from the
Geumryeongchong
Tomb

## The Wooden Boat Excavated at Wolji Pond in Gyeongju and Yeongheungdo Shipwreck, Ships of the Unified Silla Period

The Yeongheungdo Ship of Unified Silla Period is the earliest extant Korean traditional ship discovered by an underwater survey. A row of bottom plank and two levels of side planks were preserved under a pile of corroded iron caldrons. This vessel has an identical structure to the Wooden Boat of the Unified Silla Period excavated at Wolji Pond in Gyeongju. The Wooden Boat displays the developed structure of a dugout. After splitting a dugout in half, a row of bottom plank was inserted between them. Dugouts carry a high risk of capsizing due to their narrow hull. The risk of rollover can be reduced by widening the bottom of the hull by inserting extra planks there. Therefore, the bottom of the Wooden Boat consists of three planks. In order to joint these three planks, a *jangsak*, or long rectangular wooden tenon, was inserted into two points. For this, a central plank has two structures for

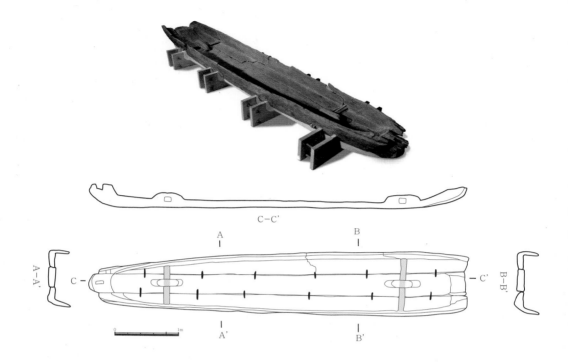

putting *jangsak*, a side plank that has mortise cuts.

The Wooden Boat and Yeongheungdo ship were used in different environments, pond and sea respectively, but they share a common structure as represented by *jangsak*. They are similar to the structure of the Goryeo shipwrecks; but vessels from both periods also have a somewhat different structure. Whereas the *jangsak* penetrate into the inside of the bottom planks, the wooden bars in these two ships are exposed.

In addition, the bottom planks and the first level of the side planks of the Yeongheungdo ship have grooves for jointing them with upper planks. This is similar to the half-lab jointing method used to build ships in the Goryeo Period.

The Wooden Boat
Excavated at Wolji
Pond in Gyeongju

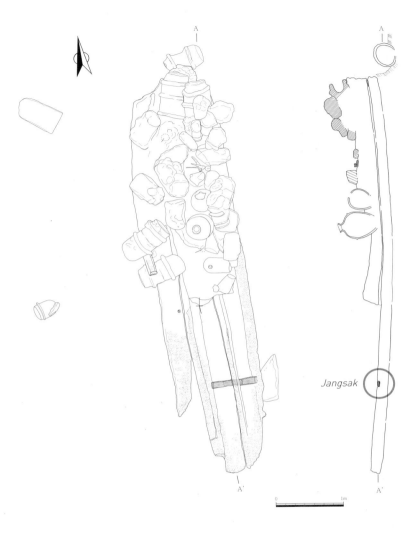

*Jangsak*

**A Hole in
the Bottom
Planks(Left) and
the First Side
Plank(Right)**

In order to joint
these planks, a
*jangsak*, i.e. a
long rectangular
wooden tenon,
was inserted into
the hole.

0                    1m

## L-shaped Chin Strake, Vestige of Dugout Canoe

So far, the wrecks of ten ships from the Goryeo Period have been found on the seafloor and mudflats of Korea. During that period, Korean traditional vessels established a unique structure and type. The L-shaped chin strake clearly shows the transition pattern of the Korean traditional vessel. It has been identified in the Yeongheungdo Shipwreck dating from the Unified Silla Period, and various Goryeo Shipwrecks, including the Sipidongpado and Wando ships, and Daebudo Shipwreck No. 2.

The L-shaped chin strake has a similar structure to both side strakes of the Wooden Boat excavated at Wolji Pond, showing the traditional pattern of the Korean dugout. The hull of the Wooden Boat that first split in two parts was inserted by a row of bottom plank between them, it was used in the transition to a bottom consisting of three or five rows of planks and side strakes consisting of several levels of planks. For example, in the case of Daebudo Shipwreck No. 2, the L-shaped chin strakes connected the bottom strakes consisting of four rows of planks and side strakes, using wooden tenons. In the case of the Dalido Shipwreck, which has no L-shaped strakes, rabbets were cut at the outer edge of the upper surface of the bottom strakes instead in order to directly connect the side planks.

The Sipidongpado and Wando Shipwrecks, which have L-shaped chin strakes, were built in the twelfth century. Except Daebudo Shipwreck No. 2, this structure has not been identified in ships of the thirteenth-fourteenth centuries, such as Mado Shipwreck Nos.

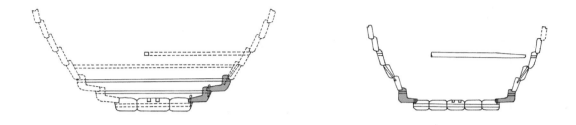

L-shaped Chin Strake of Sipidongpado Shipwreck(Left), Wando Shipwreck(Right)

L-shaped Chin
Strake of Daebudo
Shipwreck No. 2
(Upper), Dalido
Shipwreck Having
No L-shaped Chin
Strake(Lower)

1, 2 and 3 or the Anjwa and Dalido Shipwrecks.

During the Goryeo Period, the L-shaped chin stake, the last surviving vestige of a dugout, finally disappeared, and the *Hanseon* acquired its unique structure.

## Mado Shipwreck No. 4, a Tax Carrier of the Joseon Period

*Gakseon dobon*(各船圖本), a book published in the late Joseon Period, describes and explains six Joseon vessels including the *panokseon*(board-roofed ship). The book also includes an illustration of a tax carrier with two masts and yoke-shaped supports fitted to side strakes consisting of eleven levels of planks. Comparing it with the battleship depicted in this book, the tax carrier is characterized by a higher hull with fewer yoke-shaped supports, which would have enabled it to take on board more goods. In addition, the bow planks of this ship are drawn in a slanted pattern, accompanied by an explanation that the bow consists of seventeen planks laid horizontally. Mado Shipwreck No. 4, a tax carrier of the Joseon Period, has an identical structure with the tax carrier described in *Gakseon dobon*. In this ship, eleven levels of the right-hand side strakes were remaining. Grooves for the yoke-shaped supports, a structure for connecting the uppermost planks of both side strakes, were identified on the eleventh plank. Therefore, the grooves on this plank unequivocally demonstrate that it was an uppermost plank of the side strakes. It corresponds

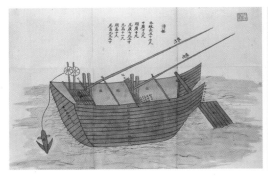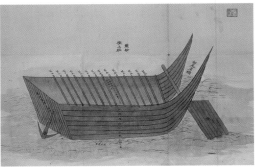

to an illustration in *Gakseon dobon*.

Mast holes were identified at two points of the bottom strake, the bow and center; and *dangappul*, i.e. wooden structures that supported a mast, were also discovered. This is the only Korean shipwreck to have two mast holes. Unlike other Korean shipwrecks whose bow strakes consisted of vertically erected planks, the bow strake of Mado Shipwreck No. 4 comprises horizontally laid wooden planks, as described in *Gakseon dobon*. Therefore, Mado Shipwreck No. 4, which lay buried under the sea for hundreds of years, confirms the actual structure of Joseon tax carriers as recorded in the historical sources.

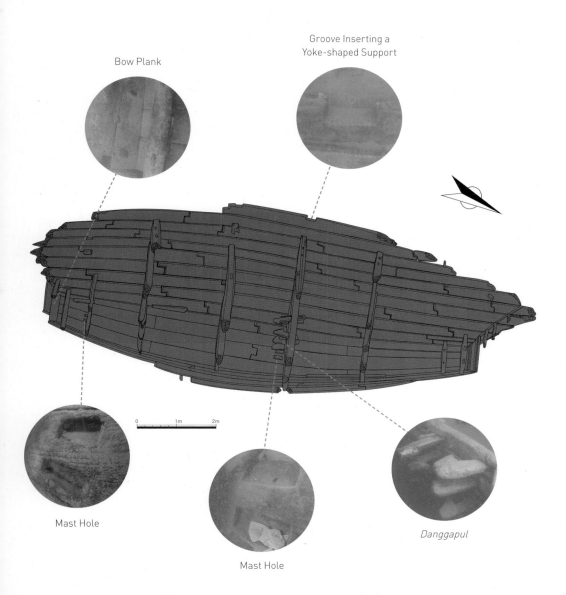

Bow Plank

Groove Inserting a
Yoke-shaped Support

Mast Hole

Mast Hole

*Danggapul*

0    1m    2m

**Hull of Mado Shipwreck No. 4**

# Wooden Tablets, Cargo Tags Found in Shipwrecks

Chapter 7

# Wooden Tablets, Cargo Tags Found in Shipwrecks

Before the invention of paper, people wrote letters and other documents on various materials such as wood, ceramic, silk, and sheepskin. Of these materials, wood was the most extensively used for a long time due to its widespread availability. The ancestors of the Korean people also wrote letters on the surface of a processed wooden tablet called a *mokgan* in Korean. Wooden tablets have been found in China and Japan as well as in Korea. In China, many bamboo slips were bound together in sequence with thread to make books. Bamboo slips have also been found in Korea; although no book of bound bamboo slips has been found.

Unlike inscriptions on tombstones, letters recording daily life were written on wooden tablets. Such tablets are extremely valuable materials that complement the scant historical sources from the early historic era. In Korea, wooden tablets provide clues about tangled historical events. Therefore, a wooden tablet is not just a piece of wood but an invaluable artifact that sheds light on the way of life and customs and practices of ancient societies.


## Wooden Tablets Found in Shipwrecks

Shipwrecks and the cargos and everyday goods contained in them can be defined as living history books that provide information on the social aspects and living conditions of vanished civilizations and societies. In order to read these "history books" accurately, certain questions need to be answered first, such as in which period was the wrecked ship active and what were its departure point and final destination. Fortunately, wooden tablets associated with shipwrecks provide the data needed to resolve such issues as these are equivalent to modern-day air bills(or sea bills), which contain such information as the sender's name and location, the recipient's name, location, and job, the nature and quantity of the shipped goods, and the date of shipment. Thus, wooden tablets record the sender's name and place, the recipient's name, place, and job, the nature and quantity of the goods, and the date.

As with the wooden tablets collected at land-based sites, those salvaged from shipwrecks are long wooden sticks measuring 15

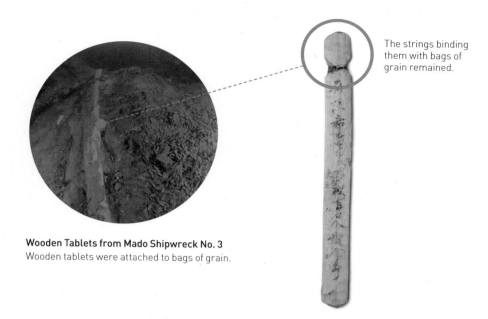

The strings binding them with bags of grain remained.

**Wooden Tablets from Mado Shipwreck No. 3**
Wooden tablets were attached to bags of grain.

to 40 centimeters in length and 1.5 to 4 centimeters in width. In order to attach them as cargo tags to cargos easily, these wooden tablets had '> <-shaped' grooves on both sides of the upper part of their body.

## Reading the Contents of Wooden Tablets

All information recorded in modern-day air bill was not recorded in wooden tablets attached to the cargos due to their size. Moreover, there was no difficulty in sending cargos when these tablets recorded the names of the recipients. Three wooden tablets bearing only the recipient's name, "Yours sincerely, the house of Choi Daegyeong," were found in the Taean Shipwreck.

Wooden tablets are usually inscribed with the recipient's name, and the nature and quantity of the shipped goods. For example, one wooden tablet contained the following: "Yours sincerely, sending from Juksan Prefecture to the house of Yun Bangjun, a military officer(*Gyowi*), in Gaegyeong, a jar of salted crab, containing four *mal*." This tablet indicates the identities of the sender(Juksan Prefecture) and the recipient(the house of Yun Bangjun), the commodity(salted crab), the storage unit(jar), and the quantity of goods(four *mal*). Another wooden tablet records the following: "A day in the Year of *Jeongmyo*, twenty-four containers of millet, each containing twenty *mal*, dispatched from Juksan Prefecture to *Jeongudongjeong* Song in Gaegyeong."

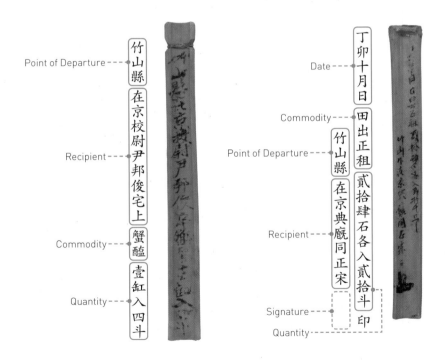

Contents Written in Wooden Tablets

In addition, the terms suggesting the relationship between senders and recipients, *taeksang*(宅上) and *hobu*(戶付), have been identified on the wooden tablets. *Taeksang*, which means 'Yours sincerely,' was used when the sender was of lower status than the recipient. When the status of the sender was equivalent to or higher than that of the recipient, the term *hobu* was written on the wooden tablets.

The wooden tablets were cargo tags. In addition to Chinese characters indicating the numbers one(一), two(二), three(三), four(四) ... ten(十), difficult characters with the same meaning, i.e. one(壹), two(貳), three(參), four(肆) ... ten(拾), were also used to prevent the falsification of the number of cargos to be shipped. In addition, a few tablets contain the signature(手決) of the sender.

## Tales Written on Wooden Tablets: Wooden Tablets from the Taean Shipwreck

Along with more than 25,000 celadon vessels, the Taean ship, a porcelain cargo ship, yielded about 20 wooden tablets containing the Chinese characters *sagi*(沙器) and *sagi*(砂器), indicating Goryeo celadon, and the recipient's name or official title, such as Choi Daegyeong, Yu Jangmyeong, *Daejeong* Insu, and An Yeong.

In addition, two wooden tablets inscribed with the word *sinhae*(辛亥: year

**Infrared Photo of a Wooden Tablet Inscribed with Chinese Characters, *Sinhae***
It is not easy to read the characters written on the wooden tablets because they were erased or dispersed in seawater. In order to read the contents of the wooden tablets, researchers take infrared photos of them and read them on a computer screen.

Wooden Tablet Found with Celadon Vessels

of the pig), the forty-eighth year of the sexagenary cycle, were also salvaged. However, it was impossible to use this to determine the exact year when the ship sank, because the cycle consists of sixty terms used to record days or years. Therefore, the research team calculated the logging date of the wooden materials used to build the ship by adopting "wiggle match" dating, a method of dating in which radiocarbon dates are matched with tree-ring dates(See Chapter 10). The results of the analysis indicate that the trees were logged sometime between 1126 and 1150(95.4 percent credibility); and the *Sinhae* year recorded on the wooden tablets is 1131. A comparison of these dates with chronological studies on porcelains revealed that the vessels found at the shipwreck were produced in the early twelfth century.

A wooden tablet found alongside the batches of celadon vessels contains the following: "Dispatch of porcelain vessels from Tamjin Prefecture to *Daejeong*(隊正) Insu(仁守) in Gaegyeong, *Jang*(長) is charge of the shipment. Signature."

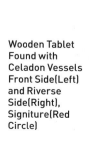

Wooden Tablet Found with Celadon Vessels Front Side(Left) and Riverse Side(Right), Signiture(Red Circle)

Tamjin Prefecture refers to present-day Gangjin in Jeollanam-do Province. *Daejeong* was the official title of the person, Insu. The back of

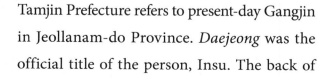

Batch of Celadon
Vessels(Left)
and Signature
on Packing
Wood(Right)

a wooden tablet is written with Chinese characters including in *jang* and a signature. *Jang* means *hojang*(戶長), the head of village officials, while *daejeong* refers to the lowest-ranking military officer in the Goryeo Period. This tablet contains the word *hobu*, which suggests that *daejeong* was not a higher rank of official than *hojang*.

The fact that the signatures are identical to those on the back of a tablet and on the packing wood of a batch of celadon vessels, demonstrates that a *hojang* in Tamjin Prefecture signed the wooden packing material and produced a cargo tag after examining the porcelain vessels for dispatch to *Daejong* Insu before the departure of the ship. The Taean Ship, which was transporting celadon vessels from Gangjin to Gaegyeong, sank off the coast of Daeseom Island in 1131.

## Wooden Tablets from Mado Shipwreck No. 1

Seventy-three wooden tablets were salvaged from Mado Shipwreck No. 1, a grain carrier. These contain information on

Wooden
Tablet Written
with Chinese
Characters,
*Jeongmyo*(Left),
Wooden
Tablet Written
with Chinese
Characters,
*Mujin*(Right)

various types of shipped goods such as rice, millet, buckwheat, bean, salted crab, and salted mackerel; and also record the point of departure of the goods, including Juksan Prefecture(present-day Haenam), Hwaejin Prefecture(present-day Naju), and Sunyeong Prefecture(present-day Jangheung), and the date of shipment, such as October and December 28, the year of *Jeongmyo*(丁卯), and January and February 19, the year of *Mujin*(戊辰).

When exactly were the *Mujin* and *Jeongmyo* years? The people mentioned on the wooden tablets, including the senders(Daesam and Songji) and the recipients(*Daejanggun* Kim Sunyeong, *Byeoljang* Kwon Geukpyeong, *Geomgyodaejanggun* Yun Gihwa, and Gyowi Yun Bangjun), provide some clues to answering this question. Of these people, Kim Sunyeong is the key to revealing the date of the shipwreck with some precision. According to *Goryeosa*(the history of Goryeo):

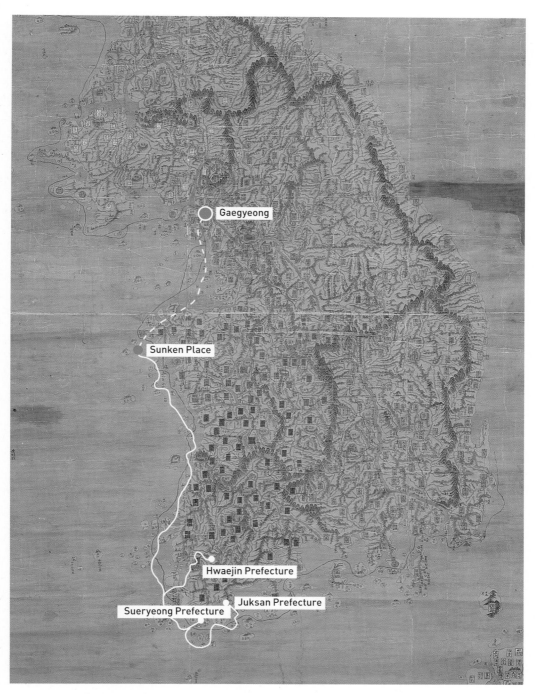

Route Taking by Mado Shipwreck No. 1(Based on the Contents of Wooden Tablets)

Wooden Tablet Marked with the Name of Kim Sunyeong

In the second year of the reign of King Sinjong, Kim Sunyeong informed Choe Chungheon, a military ruler, about the infiltration of Kim Jungeo, his son-in-law, a rebel, into Gaegyeong... He was appointed to the post of *Janggun*(general).

He was appointed to *Janggun*(general) in 1199. The official rank of Kim Sunyeong is mentioned in *Daejanggun*(great general) in the wooden tablets. Therefore, it can be ascertained that the *Mujin* and *Jeongmyo* years were 1207 AD and 1208 AD, respectively. Mado Shipwreck No. 1 yielded a number of objects that have enabled us to infer the measurement unit of the Goryeo Period. Since the upper part of a wooden tablet recording the following: "Yours sincerely, sending two jars containing five *mal* each to the house of *Geomgyodaejanggun* Yun Gihwa," was broken, it was

The Name of Kim Sunyeong Recorded in *Goryeosa* Vol. 129

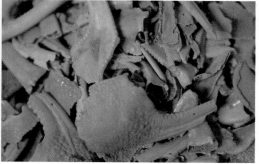

impossible to determine the nature of the goods contained in the jars or the sender's name. However, this tag was found with two stoneware jars containing salted shrimp and salted crab, respectively. As the volume of these two jars is about 18 liters, and the tag records that one jar contained five *mal*, we can assume indirectly the volume of one *mal* in the Goryeo Period.

Two Stoneware Jars Found with Wooden Tablet Bearing the Name of Yun Gihwa(Left), Crabs Contained in a Jar(Right)

## Wooden Tablets from Mado Shipwreck No. 2

As with Mado Shipwreck No. 1, Mado Shipwreck No. 2 was a grain carrier. The discovery of forty-seven wooden tablets in the hull suggest that the ship was loaded with rice, soybeans, yeast, and salted fish that were being shipped from Musong, Gochang and Jangsa Prefectures(present-day Gochang) and Gobu Country(present-day Jeongeup) to officials in Gaegyeong, namely, *Nangjung* Lee Geukseo, *Daegyeong* Yu, and *Jungbangdojanggyeo* Oh Munbu.

Although none of the wooden tablets was written with the year of the sexagenary cycle, the date of the shipwreck could be inferred

Wooden Tablet Marked with the Name of Yun Gihwa

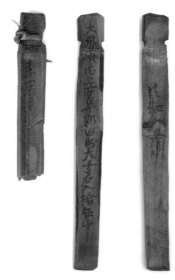

Wooden Tablet Marked with the Name of Lee Geukseo(Left), Front and Reverse Sides of a Wooden Tablet Inscribed with the Chinese Characters, *Daegyeong* Yu (Center, Right)

from the names of the people recorded on them.

According to *Goryeosa* Lee Geukseo, a *Chumilwonbusa*, attacked rebel troops in Uiju in the sixth year of King Gojong's reign(1219); and was subsequently appointed to the rank of *Pyeongjangsa* in the seventh year of King Gojong's reign(1220). Thus, as *Nangjung*(upper fifth rank) was a lower official rank than *Chumilwonbusa*(upper third rank), it can be inferred that this ship sailed towards Gaegyeong before 1219, the year in which he was appointed to the rank of *Chumilwonbusa*. The date of the shipwreck can also be deduced through the other person mentioned on the wooden tablets, *Daegyeong* Yu. Mado

Front and Reverse Sides of a Wooden Tablet(Left), Celadon Prunus Vase with Inlaid Design(Right)

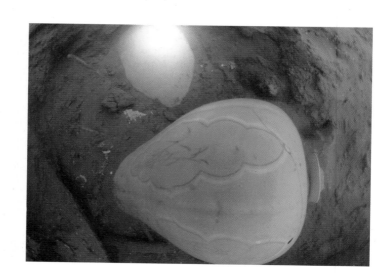

Ship No. 2 was loaded in Gochang and its neighboring place with goods destined for Gaegyeong. During the Goryeo Period, the Musong Yu family was based in this area. One of its members, Yu Jaryang(1150-1229), was appointed to the position of *Daegyeong* before retiring in 1213. Therefore, it can be inferred that this ship was wrecked before 1213.

In addition, wooden tablets were attached to the necks of two celadon prunus vases, each inscribed with the phrase "Yours sincerely, sending to *Jungbangdojanggyeo* Oh Munbu, containing sesame oil in a vase" and "Yours sincerely, sending to *Jungbangdojanggyeo* Oh Munbu, containing high quality honey in a vase" respectively. Before It has been kwon that prunus vase was the liquor bottle before the discovery of them. However, these wooden tablets revealed that they were also used to contain sesame oil and honey. Due to their high academic value, these two prunus vases

Celadon Prunus Vase with Incised Design(Left), Front and Reverse Sides of a Wooden Tablet(Right)

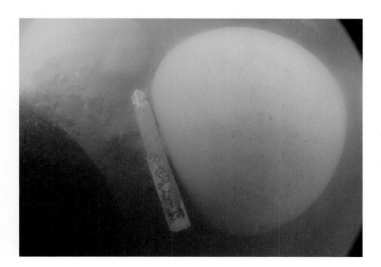

were designated as a Treasure in Korea. In addition, these tablets also indicate that prunus vases were inscribed with the Chinese character *jun*(樽) in the Goryeo Period.

## Wooden Tablets from Mado Shipwreck No. 3

Along with various goods including grains, hemp cloth, and antlers, thirty-five wooden tablets were salvaged from Mado Shipwreck No. 3. As with Mado Shipwreck No. 2, none of the wooden tablets found in this shipwreck was inscribed with the year of the sexagenary cycle. Nevertheless, the date of the shipwreck could be inferred from the names of the people recorded on the wooden tablets.

Front and Reverse Sides of a Wooden Tablet Marked with the Name of Sin Yunhwa

For example, one wooden tablet contains the expression: "Yours sincerely, sending to the house of *Sirang* Shin Yunhwa, a jar of salted abalone." Shin Yunhwa, who joined the coup d'état that subverted the military regime of the House of Choe in the *Muo* year(1258), was appointed to the rank of *Janggun*(general). He was dispatched as an envoy of Goryeo to the Mongol Empire in the first year of King Wonjong's reign(1260). *Sirang* was the same official rank as *janggun* in Goryeo, i.e. the upper fourth rank. Therefore, it can be assumed that the ship sank around 1260.

Another wooden tablet contains the expression: "Yours sincerely, sending to the house of *Seungje* Yu, a *gonegi*(古乃只) of salted abalone." A *seungje* was a secretary in charge of receiving and delivering the king's orders. Yu Cheonu is known to have occupied the post of *seungje* from around 1260 to 1268.

One wooden tablet written with "Yours sincerely, sending to the house of *Sasim* Kim *Yeonggong*. a jar of salted mussels, containing five *mal* in each jar, Heonrye." Kim *Yeonggong* refers to Kim Jun, a military ruler. The title of *Yeonggong* was the most honorary term for an emperor. Kim Jun, who was a slave, was the leader of the coup d'état that took place in the *Muo* year(1257). He killed Choe Ui and became the supreme authority. He was appointed *Sijung*(prime minister) and was raised to *Haeyanghu*(which roughly translated as Earl of *Haeyang*) in the sixth year of King Wonjong's reign(1265). Thereafter, he was granted the title of *Yeonggong*.

These records suggest that Mado Ship No. 3 sank off the Sea around Mado Island sometime between 1265 and 1268.

One of the noticeable words recorded on the wooden tablets is *jutaeksang*(主宅上), which was a higher honorific term than *taeksang*(宅上). The tags on the cargos sent to Kim Jun are inscribed not with the word *taeksang* but with *jutaeksang*, as are tags on the

Front and Reverse Sides of a Wooden Tablet Inscribed with the Chinese Characters, Yu *Seungje*

The tablet was discovered when silt was removed a stoneware jar(Left), the stoneware jar (Right)

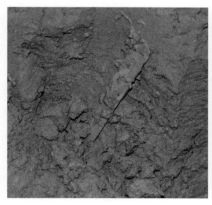

Front and Reverse sides of a Wooden Tablet Inscribed with the Chinese Characters, Kim *Yeonggong*

A stoneware jar found near the wooden tablet sending to Kim Jun containing byssuses of mussel.

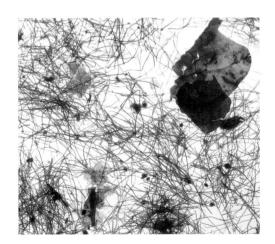

cargo sent to Kim *Sirang*. The person who sent the cargos to them was named Heonrye. It has been assumed that Kim *Sirang* was one of the members of Kim Jun's family, possibly one of his sons who served as a *sirang*(civil servant).

One cargo tag sent to Kim Jun contains the Chinese characters, *sasim*(事審). In order to control local powers, the Goryeo Dynasty appointed high-ranking officials in the central government to the *sasim* in their hometowns. The *sasim* had the right to appoint local officials under the *buhojang*(副戶長), but also had joint responsibility for any events, such as revolts, occurring within his jurisdiction. Kim Jun received the salted mussels from the province where he was appointed to the post of *sasim*.

The title of *sasim* has also been identified on another wooden tablet, as follows: "Yours sincerely, sending to the house of the *Busasim*(副事審) of Yeosu Prefecture, seven *mal* of hulled barley, supervising shipping, *Seungdongjeong* Oh, signature." Here, the word *busasim* refers to the vice-*sasim*. Mado Ship No. 3 departed from Yeosu carrying a shipment of hulled barley destined for the *busasim* of this prefecture.

In addition to high officials, several cargo tags record the names of the offices, such as the *Jeonminbyenjeongdogam*(田民辨正都監: Institute for the Prevention of Private Acquisition of Public Taxation Land or Rights), *Jungbang*(重房: Supreme Council),

**Wooden Tablet and Its Front and Reverse Sides Inscribed with the Chinese Characters, Yeosuhyeon** *Busasim*
It was found buried in grain.

*Sambyeolcho*(三別抄: Special Military Unit), and *Dogwan*(都官: Bureau for the Registration and Management of Slaves), as the recipients of cargos including dried mussels, hemp *cloth*, dog meat jerky, and fish oils. Mado Ship No 3, which was bound for Ganghwado Island, a temporary capital, was loaded with goods destined for Kim Jun

**Wooden Tablet and Its Front and Reverse Sides Inscribed with the Chinese Characters,** *Usambeonbyeolcho*
This is a cargo tag attached to a bag containing mussels.

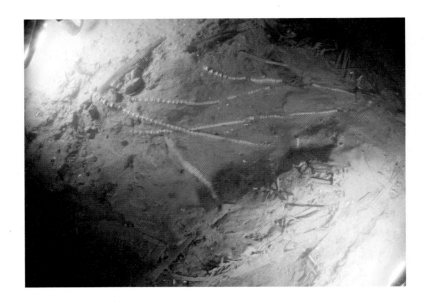

Bamboo Box Containing Shark Bones(Left), Front and Reverse Sides of a Wooden Tablet Inscribed with the Chinese Characters, *Usambeonbyeolcho* and *Doryeong*(Right)

and his men, and the offices they served. Ultimately, this giant puzzle, consisting of a ship transporting cargos for a powerful figure of the Goryeo military regime and his party, could only be completed thanks to the records written on wooden tablets.

## Wooden Tablets and 'Buncheong' Vessels from Mado Shipwreck No. 4

Mado Shipwreck No. 4 was the first shipwreck dating the Joseon Period to be found in Korea. This was a cargo vessel transporting taxes paid in the form of grains and goods. The ship's skillfully made hull and its large cargo of grain suggest that it could have been a government-run tax carrier. The discovery of wooden tablets written with the Chinese characters *Najugwangheungchang*(羅州廣興倉) confirmed this fact.

Of the sixty-three wooden tablets salvaged from the wreck, fifty-four contain the word *Najugwangheungchang*. Here, Naju(羅州) refers to present-day Naju in Jeollanam-do Province, while the Gwangheungchang(廣興倉) was a tax warehouse of the Joseon Period that also paid a stipend to government officials. The Gwangheungchang located in present-day Mapo in Seoul was the final destination of all tax carriers during the Joseon Period. Comparative studies on the contents of wooden tablets salvaged from Goryeo shipwrecks and Mado Shipwreck No. 4(Joseon) implicitly show the different characteristics of the two periods.

Whereas wooden tablets are the only objects that enable us to infer the dates of Goryeo shipwrecks such as Mado Shipwrecks Nos. 1, 2 and 3, Mado Shipwreck No. 4 has yielded other objects, namely *buncheong* wares, which enable us to calculate the date this ship sank. Of the 155 *buncheong* vessels salvaged from this site, three are inscribed with the Chinese characters, *naeseom*(內贍). Here, *Naeseom* refers to the *Naeseomsi*(內贍寺), a government

Wooden Tablet Inscribed with the Chinese Characters, *Najugwang-heungchang*

institute responsible for managing tribute payments to the royal family, bestowing liquors and foods on high-ranking officials, and dispatching foods and textiles to the Jurchens and Japanese. According to *The Annals of the Joseon Dynasty*(朝鮮王朝實錄), King Taejong ordered the marking on

Wooden Tablets Inscribed with the Chinese Characters, *Najugwangheungchang*, from Mado Shipwreck No. 4

porcelain and wooden vessels the names of the institutions that possessed them in 1417, while King Sejong ordered the marking of the names of the producers on tribute vessels in 1421. The fact that only the name of the relevant government institution was stamped on *buncheong* vessels carried by this cargo vessel, it was wrecked sometime between 1417 and 1421.

To sum up, *buncheong* vessels inscribed with the Chinese character, *naeseom*, demonstrate that the ship sank between 1417 and 1421. Considering the Chinese characters on the wooden tablets and the *buncheong* wares, this was almost certainly a cargo ship carrying grains and ceramic vessels destined for the Gwangheungchang in Hanyang, until it was wrecked off the Sea around Mado Island.

*Buncheong* Vessels Stamped with Chinese Characters, *Naeseom*

It appears that Mado Shipwrecks Nos. 1, 2 and 3 were transporting goods sent by private individuals to other private individuals or government offices, leaving it unclear as to whether they were government-run tax carriers or not. However, the wooden tablets records only the recipient of the cargo, *Najugwangheungchang*, in other words the government-run tax warehouse in Naju, constitute definite proof that Mado Shipwreck No. 4 was a government-run tax carrier.

# Sailors, the Heroes of Tragic Shipwrecks

## Chapter 8

# Sailors, the Heroes of Tragic Shipwrecks

On 29 May 2008, when the excavation of the Taean Shipwreck, a porcelain carrier, came to an end, special artifacts
were found on the seafloor at a depth of 15 meters. These
were the skeletal remains of a man, including the left and right
shoulder blades, the left humerus, the left and right ulnae, and the
spine.

The man would have been about 160 centimeters tall, had the
highly developed arm and backbone indicative of a life of manual
labor. Considering that no traces of fractures or diseases were
detected in his bones, he was likely a very healthy sailor. Why did
such a healthy sailor take his last sleep in the sea?

**Skeletal Remains of a Dead Man Found under Batches of Porcelain Vessels from the Taean Shipwreck**
These are the skeletal remains of a man about 30 years old. He appears to have been trapped and crushed under falling vessels while the ship was sinking.

When his bones were found, his right arm was stretched, and his shoulder blades and spine were slightly curved to the left. It seems that he was striving to raise his upper body while wrenching to his left to escape from the inflow of water as the ship was sinking. In spite of his desperate struggle to escape from falling cargos, particularly porcelain vessels, he eventually shared the fate of the ship.

Although fragments of skull were found in the Shinan Shipwreck, this was the first time that human skeletal remains had been recovered from a Korean shipwreck. As all the hulls of Korean shipwrecks have been found near the coast, it is likely there were few casualties of such accidents because the crews could easily reach nearby lands and islands. Sadly, this man appears to have died beneath the falling cargo.

Shipwrecks contain many items used by sailors as well as human skeletal remains. The next chapter will look at life on board Korean ships through the objects used and possessed by sailors.

## People on Board Shipwrecks

Who were the crew of these shipwrecks? How many sailors were on board? *the Goryeosa*(the history of Goryeo) and bronze spoons salvaged from shipwrecks have provided some clues to the answers to these questions. The Article of Marine Transportation(漕運條), Food and Money(食貨) referred to in the *Goryeosa*(Vol. 79) provides for compensation of damages related to a cargo vessel shipping carrying grains and goods to be paid as taxes, as follows:

> If the ship departed on time, but sank in a storm along with the grain tax, more than three *chogong*(梢工) , and five *suin*(水手) and *japin*(雜人), the grain tax will not be re-levied. However, if the ship did not depart on time, chogong and susu were drowned up to one third, the tax will be levied on the *saekjeon*(色典), *chogong* and *susu* belonging to the office with which the ship is registered.

Here, the *saekjeon* was an official in the local tax storehouse who supervised the crews on board a cargo fleet at sea, and checked the quantity of cargos and managed the stocking thereof while the ships were anchored at Gyeongchang, the tax warehouse in Gaegyeong, the final destination of a fleet. The *chogong* was the captain who commanded the navigation of a cargo vessel. He was also in charge of the cargos. The *suin* were rowers and japin were porters. In general, a fleet supervised under one or two *saekjeon* consisted of six cargo vessels in the Goryeo Period, and each ship had a crew of between eleven and fourteen sailors, including a chogong and a dozen or so *suin* and *japin*.

Bronze spoons salvaged from shipwrecks are crucial materials with which to infer the number of crew members of a ship. Most

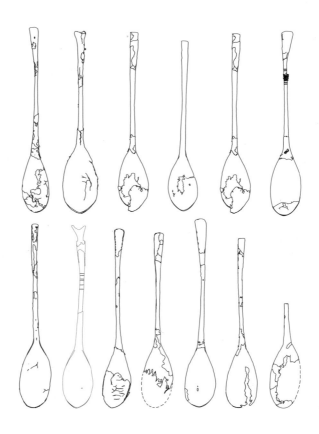

Bronze Spoons
from Mado
Shipwreck No. 1

remaining Goryeo bronze spoons have been found in tombs; but
the underwater excavations of Goryeo shipwrecks have yielded
a number of them, such as the thirteen spoons recovered from
Mado Shipwreck No. 1, the twelve from Mado Shipwreck No. 2,
and nine from Mado Shipwreck No. 3. Even after considering
the possibility that some spoons were lost, the number of
bronze spoons on a ship was probably fewer than fifteen, which
corresponds to the number of crew members assumed by other
studies of historical sources.

Various historical sources from the Joseon Period describe the
number of crew members of a fleet more clearly than those

published during the Goryeo Period. *Hanghaeilgi*(航海日記) is a ship's log written by Jo Hibaek, a governor of Hamyeol Prefecture and a chief tax collector at the *Seongchangdang*(聖堂倉), a tax storehouse formerly located in present-day Seondang-myeon, Iksan, Jeollabuk-do Province. This log records the voyage of a fleet consisting of sixteen cargo vessels carrying 16,000 *seoks* of grain collected in eight prefectures in Jeolla-do Province that departed from Ungpo in Jeollabuk-do Province on 23 March 1875 and arrived at Seoul on 18 April 1875. The log is also called *Johaengilrok*(漕行日錄) or *Eulhaejohaengrok*(乙亥漕行錄).

According to this log, the fleet consisted of twelve cargo vessels and 228 crew members. Aside from him and his servants and local officials, the crews were composed of twelve ship's mates(one per ship) and 180 sailors(fifteen per ship). Therefore, it can be assumed that the crew of a cargo ship was composed of around 18-19 people in the Joseon Period. In fact, cargo ships of the Joseon Period had slightly larger crews than those of the Goryeo Period as they were about 1.3 times larger.

## Living Space for Sailors

Given that the number of people on board numbered between ten and twenty, how did they pass the time and survive the long voyage? According to *Eulhaejohaengrok*, it took 26 days to sail from the Geumgang River estuary to Mapo in Seoul, and the crew remained on board for most of that time.

The Goryeo shipwrecks salvaged during underwater excavations sailed a greater distance than the fleet mentioned in *Eulhaejohaengrok*. They planned a 20 to 30 day voyage from the Yeongsangang River estuary to Gaegyeong(Mado Shipwreck No. 1), from Gomsoman Bay in Buan to Gaegyeong(Mado Shipwreck No. 2), and from Yeosu to Ganghwado Island(Mado Shipwreck No. 3). Where were the cargos loaded in the hull and how did the crews live on a ship? The objects salvaged from the shipwrecks provide some clues to such questions.

When we observe the hull of Mado Shipwreck No. 3, the most

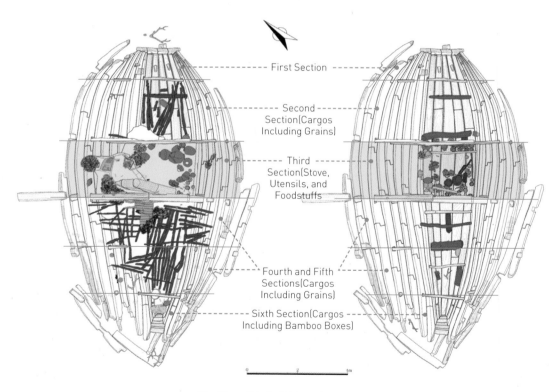

First Section

Second Section(Cargos Including Grains)

Third Section(Stove, Utensils, and Foodstuffs)

Fourth and Fifth Sections(Cargos Including Grains)

Sixth Section(Cargos Including Bamboo Boxes)

The Plan of Mado Shipwreck No. 3

intact of the Goryeo shipwrecks excavated to date, we observed that *garyong*(beam) that joints right and left side planks divide the space under the upper deck into six partitions. Items of equipment such as an anchor windlass were installed on the steeply-sloping first partition built into the bow. Cargos including grains were shipped in the second, fourth and fifth partitions. The illustration shows that wooden supports were laid on the floor to prevent water from penetrating the cargos. The sixth partition under the stern was a very closed space loaded with bamboo boxes containing shark bones and stoneware jars containing salted fish. A stove was installed in the left part of the third partition, the center of the ship where the mast was fixed. Two caldrons, dishes

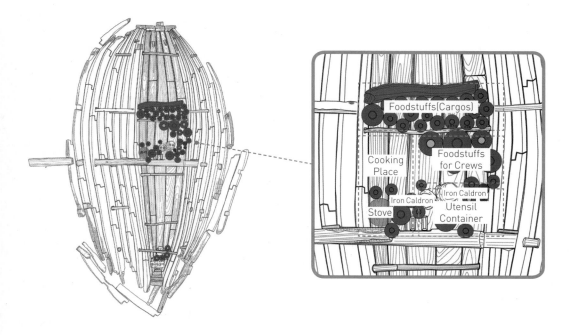

Stove from the Third Partition and Objects Found Around It from Mado Shipwreck No. 1

'*Segokunbanseon*
(Cargo Vessel of
Tax Paid as Grain),'
Yu Unhong
(1797-1859) and
'*Fishing Boat*'
(Unknown Author)

and stoneware jars containing side dishes for sailors were found around the stove; and stoneware jars containing salted fish(cargo) were also loaded in the third partition, the space in which the goods for the sailors were stored.

The hull structure of other salvaged Korean ships, including the Sipidongpado Shipwreck and Mado Shipwreck Nos. 1, 2 and 4, is similar to that of Mado Shipwreck No. 3. The space under the upper deck was used to store the supplies and possessions of the sailors. It was about 2 meters long and 1 meter wide, sufficiently large to permit the sailors to cook there. It seems that the crew slept and ate food on the upper deck and other upper structures. However, it was impossible to detect any other traces of the life led by the sailors because the space had been swept away by waves and tidal currents.

The sailors' life on board ship can be inferred from paintings produced in the Joseon Period. Yu Unhong's painting *Segokun-*

*banseon*(Cargo Vessel Carrying Tax Paid as Grain) depicts a vessel without a deck, with a hull full of grain containers. Meanwhile, a *minwha*(fork painting) by an unknown artist depicts a vessel with a facility covered with a thatched roof.

> According to *Eulhaejohaengrok*(乙亥漕行錄):
> Watching all sides after removing cover, I was uttering an exclamation.
> I was lying on a ship for sleeping. I was distressed because four ships have not yet arrived.

This describes how the crew on board a ship slept in a facility with a cover or roof. It was possible that this was a fixed facility of some sort, although it can be also assumed that it was a temporary arrangement due to the narrowness of the deck.

## Preparing and Eating Food on the Ship

How did sailors prepare and eat food while confined in a narrow space during a turbulent voyage? Various objects that provide clues to this question have been found in the sunken hulls. Iron caldrons and steamers were found around the stoves of the Goryeo shipwrecks. Sailors probably had to cook very carefully in order to prevent sparks from their fire setting fire to the ships. Stones for fire prevention were found in the kitchen in the Sipidongpado and Anjwa Shipwrecks, and in Mado Shipwreck Nos. 1, 2, 3 and 4; while pine cones and burned woods assumed to be fuel were identified in Mado Shipwreck Nos. 1 and 4.

Pine Cones from Mado Shipwreck No. 1(Left) and Stone Slab of a Stove Found in the Sipidongpado Shipwreck(Right)

In the shipwrecks, various cooking utensils including iron caldrons and earthenware steamers were found around a stove. For example, Mado Shipwreck No. 1 contained a steamer and two iron caldrons, one of which appears to be a large, deep cooker. It

seems that the steamer was placed on the caldron to cook cereals. According to historical sources published in the Three Kingdoms Period, people steamed rice rather than boiling it. It seems that the tradition of steaming grain survived into the Goryeo Period. The fact that textiles aimed at preventing the escape of grains were

Iron Caldrons and a Steamer from Mado Shipwreck No. 1

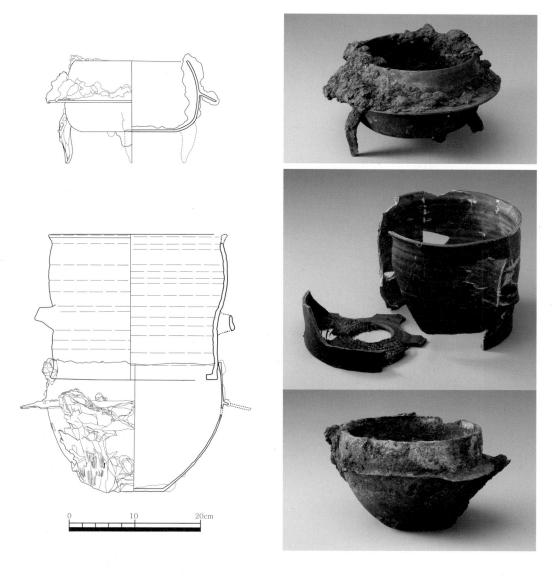

0        10        20cm

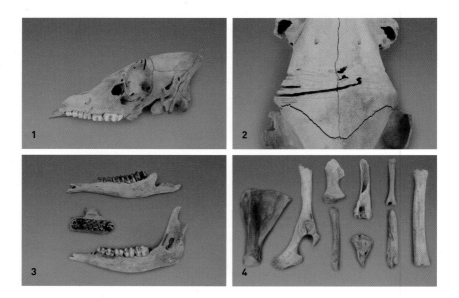

attached to the bottom of the steamer demonstrates that it was a cooker used on ship. The other caldron, which has legs, may have be used to cook soups, stews and side dishes.

One of the interesting facts here is that the volume of a steamer is about 9 liters. Considering that a modern rice cooker for five people is about 1 liter(i.e. 0.2 liters per person), this cooker would have served about 40-45 people by current standards. Korean people had a reputation for being voracious eaters in the pre-modern era: "An adult man eats two meals a day. He eats seven *hop*(1 *hop*: 0.18 liter) at each meal." It seems that a crew member did not eat even seven *hop* of rice per day; but he might have eaten 2-3 times more than a modern adult man. Considering this assumption, a steamer was a cooker for 15-22 men, and almost corresponds to the number of people on board.

What kinds of food did sailors eat? It is difficult to determine which was the main grain they consumed, i.e. rice, or barley, or millet. The sunken hull was found to contain large quantities of rice, barley, millet and soybeans; but these were cargos rather than food supplies for the crew. Nevertheless, various animal remains assumed to be food for the sailors were salvaged from

Skulls and Jawbones of Rats from Mado Shipwreck No. 3

the hull. In the case of Mado Shipwreck No. 2, bones of various species, including pig(30 pieces), deer(31 pieces), dog, cow, elk, duck, chicken, and cormorant, were collected from the hull. On six pig skulls, there are traces of a blow left by an instrument. It seems that these skulls were related to ritual prayers for a safe voyage.

In addition, Mado Shipwreck No. 3, a grain cargo, also yielded mammal bones, which include 39 pig bones(43.3 percent), 30 deer bones(33.3 percent), two elk bones, five cow bones and three rat bones. Judging by the traces of cutting visible on some of these bones, these were foodstuffs eaten by the people on board. Of course, the rats might not have been eaten as food. Whereas lots of pig skulls were found in Mado Shipwreck No. 2, various other pig bones were salvaged from Mado Shipwreck No. 3, which suggests that these were daily goods rather than sacrificial offerings. We can assume that the people on the ship ate diverse meats such as pig, deer and dog.

About 120 stoneware jars were salvaged from the Goryeo

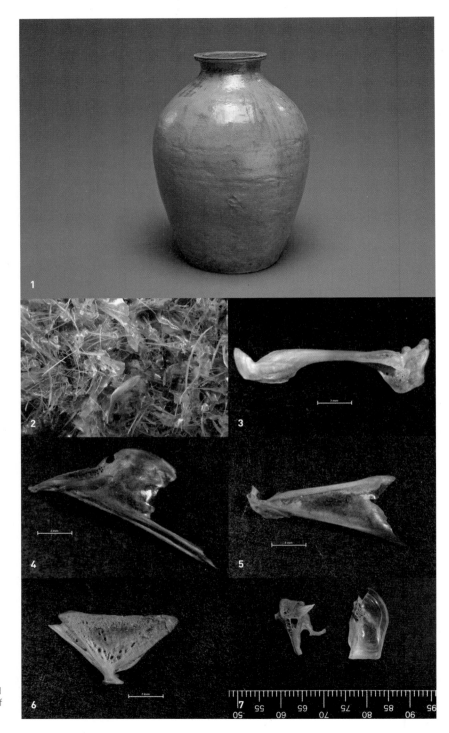

**Stoneware Jar from Mado Shipwreck No. 3**

This jar contained a large quantity of gizzard bones.

**Stoneware Jar from Mado Shipwreck No. 3**

This jar contained a mixture of bones of small fish including herring, gizzard, large-eyed herring, and croaker, and a fragment of a bronze spoon.

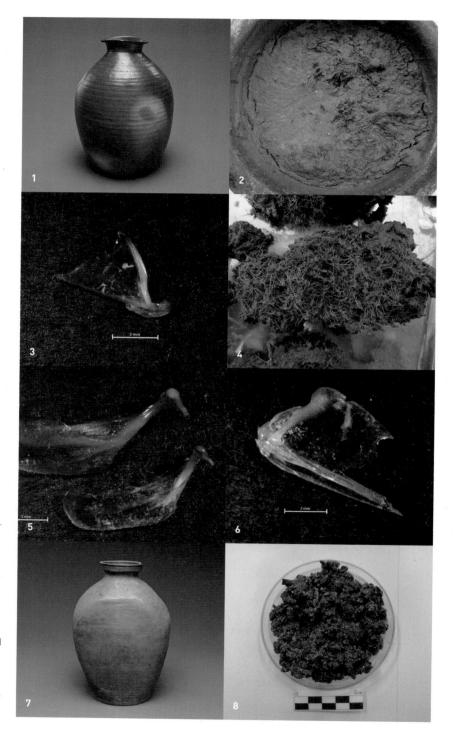

**Stoneware Flat Jar Containing Contents Assumed to be Salted Fish from Mado Shipwreck No. 3**

The mouth of this jar was sealed with herbal plants. The jar contained a large quantity of various small fish bones(1~6).

**Contents of a Stoneware Jar from Mado Shipwreck No. 3**

The mouth of this jar was also sealed by herbal plants. The jar contained contents assumed to be fermented soybean paste (7~8).

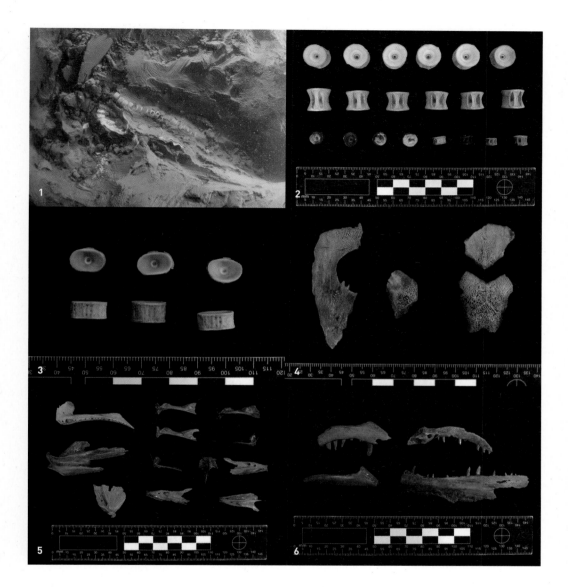

Shipwrecks in total. The jars themselves were not cargos, but rather containers for storing water, salted fish, fermented vegetables (*kimchi*) and fermented soybean paste(*doenjang*). More than thirty stoneware jars were salvaged from the third partition of Mado Shipwreck No. 3, some of which contained fish bones. Each jar

**Fish Bones Found at the Center of Mado Shipwreck No.3.**
While stoneware jars contained the bones of small and larger fishes, including shark, dogfish shark, gurnard, sea-bream, croaker, and hairtail, were loaded in this part of the ship.

Large Jars from
Mado Shipwreck
No. 2

contained a mixture of bones of small fish including herring, gizzard, large-eyed herring, and croaker. As these fish spoil easily, they could be the remains of salted fermented fish that were mixed with various species of small fish. Most of these vessels were salvaged intact, and even contain contents such as salted fish and fermented soy products. The stoneware jars vary in size, though most have a capacity of less than 30 liters(95 percent), whereas the water jars have a capacity of more than 120 liters, as water is of course an absolute necessity during a sea voyage.

*Eulhaejohaengrok* states that the fleet put in at Yeongheungdo Island on April 4th by the lunar calendar, twelve days out from its departure, to take on fresh supplies of water. According to *Yuamchongseo*(柳菴叢書), due to their deep draft, the heavily laden cargo vessels could not weigh anchor in the port. Therefore, small boats called *geodoseon*(居刀船) brought fuel for cooking and water to them. The large jars found in the Mado Shipwreck Nos. 1 and

2 may have been used to store water collected on land or supplied by the *geodoseon*.

Lastly, this chapter will discuss the tableware and cooking implements used by the crew, including bronze(utensils), stoneware and porcelain vessels. The table below classifies the utensils salvaged from Mado Shipwreck Nos. 1, 2 and 3, and shows that celadon vessels account for the majority of utensils used by the people on board. Most of the celadon vessels used by sailors were low-quality

| Shipwreck | | Mado No. 1 | Mado No. 2 | Mado No. 3 | Total |
|---|---|---|---|---|---|
| Bronze | Bowls with Lid | | | 2 | 2 |
| | Bowls | | 2 | 20 | 22 |
| | Dishes | | 1 | 9 | 10 |
| | Spoons | 13 | 12 | 9 | 34 |
| | Chopstick | | | 4 (two sets) | 4 |
| | Ladles | | | 1 | 1 |
| Celadon | Vases | 3 | 4 | | 7 |
| | Bowls | 37 | 17 | 9 | 63 |
| | Dishes | 60 | 24 | 9 | 93 |
| | Bowls(Type 'wan') | | 1 | 1 | 2 |
| | Cups | 7 | 3 | 3 | 13 |
| Stoneware | Bottles | 2 | | 4 | 6 |
| | Dishes | 4 | | 1 | 5 |
| | Bowls(Type 'wan') | 2 | | | 2 |
| Wood and Bamboo | Chopsticks | 13 | 28 | 9 | 50 |
| | Cupstands | | 1 | | 1 |
| Total | | 141 | 93 | 81 | 315 |

Utensils from Mado Shipwreck Nos. 1, 2 and 3

goods lacking any decorative features, perhaps reflecting their low social status.

Since the number of bronze spoons is relatively high, it seems that even sailors used spoons made of bronze. Except for Mado Shipwreck No. 3, only a few bronze utensils were excavated. As bronze vessels were of a higher grade than celadon vessels, high-ranking crew members may have used these items. Bronze chopsticks were only found in Mado Shipwreck No. 3(two sets), whereas most of the other salvaged shipwrecks have yielded bamboo and wooden chopsticks; and few stoneware vessels have been salvaged from any shipwrecks. Therefore, it may be assumed that each member of a ship's crew had one or two dishes, one spoon, and a set of chopsticks as personal items; while three to five people might have shared a bottle.

**Sets of Bronze Utensils from Goryeo Shipwrecks**
1 Bowl with a Lid
2 Dish
3 Dish
4 Bowl
5 Chopsticks and a Spoon

**Sets of Utensils
from Goryeo
Shipwrecks**
**1** Celadon Bottle
**2** Celadon Dish
**3** Celadon Bowl
**4** Stoneware Dish
**5** Celadon Bowl
**6** Bronze Spoon
**7** Bamboo
  Chopsticks

Given that Mado Shipwreck No. 3 sank in the 1260s, during the late phase of the Mongol invasion of Goryeo when its economy was close to ruin, it is hard to imagine that ordinary seamen used bronze utensils.

In contrast with other Goryeo Shipwrecks containing small quantities of bronze utensils and large quantities of low-quantity celadon vessels, the number of bronze utensils found on Mado Shipwreck No. 3 is higher than that of celadon vessels. Apart from the spoons, bronze utensils account for about fifty percent of all the utensils found in Mado Shipwreck No. 3, in other words, ten times more than on Mado Shipwreck No. 2 (3 pieces, 4 percent); while no bronze utensils at all were salvaged from Mado Shipwreck No. 1. Moreover, this ship contained two bronze bowls with a lid and two sets of bronze chopsticks, while none were found on any other Goryeo shipwrecks. As explained in the previous chapter's discussion on the contents of wooden tablets, this ship contained cargos sent to Kim Jun, a military ruler in the period 1258-1268, by Kim Sirang, a relative of Kim Jun, and offices related to his regime, which include the *Jeonminbyeonjeongdogam*(田民辨正都監: Institute for Preventing the Private Acquisition of Public Taxation Land or Rights), the *Jungbang*(重房: Supreme Council), the *Sambyeolcho*(Special Military Unit of the Right), and the *Dogwan*(都官: Bureau for the Registration and Management of Slaves). In other words, this was a cargo vessel transporting goods to the most powerful man in Goryeo and the institutes controlled by him. The utensils of the crew found in this shipwreck reflect these circumstances.

It seems that the utensils were not actually personal belongings but items furnished by the institute. It is possible that Mado Shipwreck No. 3 was a large ship with good equipment, and formed part of a large fleet. The discovery of the two sets of bronze bowls with a lid and the chopsticks raises the possibility that two officials who were in charge of the fleet were aboard this ship. The fact that large quantities of bronze utensils were identified in this shipwreck might reflect it.

## ● Special Cargo from Mado Shipwreck No. 3 ●

Mado Shipwreck No. 3 contained many unique items that have not been discovered in other Goryeo shipwrecks. Among the most representative of these items are a wooden saddlebow and a bronze horse bell; although other unusual items such as ornaments used to adorn the straps of *gat*(traditional Korean hats made of bamboo and horsehair) and *paeraengi*(rough hats made of bamboo braid that were worn by mourners), also called jukyeong, were also found on the ship. In pre-modern Korea, a hat symbolized social status. For instance, people above the rank of local officials could wear a hat. Also discovered were two Chinese coins, a *xiangfuyuanbao*(祥符元寶) cast in 1008-1016 AD and a *zhihetongbao*(至和通寶) cast in 1054-1056 AD. Similar Chinese coins are frequently excavated from Goryeo tombs, as Chinese coins were in circulation in Gaegyeong during that period. Nobles above the rank of local officials might also have carried Chinese coins. As such, the discovery of the Chinese coins, *jukyeong* hat, saddlebow and bronze horse bell suggests that officials in charge of the fleet were aboard Mado Shipwreck No. 3.
Chess(*janggi*) pieces are among the other interesting items found at Mado Shipwreck No. 3.

Chess was introduced to Korea from the Song Dynasty of China in the early Goryeo Period. Given that the ship sank in the 1260s, these pieces constitute one of the earliest artifacts related with Korean chess. Of the forty-seven chess pieces made of flat pebbles, several are inscribed with a Chinese character such as *cha*(車), *po*(砲) and *jol*(卒).

Wooden Saddlebow

Jukyeong

Xiangfuyuanbao

Zhihetongbao

Bronze Horse Bell

Chess Pieces

# • Items Used by Sailors •

In addition to the various items related to cooking and eating, the shipwrecks contained many everyday items such as adzes, sword handles, various types of bamboo boxes, net bags and combs.

## Tools and Whetstones

Several types of tools have been found in the submerged hulls, including wooden hammers, sword handles, adz hafts, and the handles of *josae*, a tool for harvesting oysters.

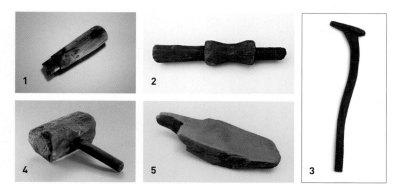

## Bamboo Basket from Mado Shipwreck No. 3

A wooden basket from Tomb No. 1, dated to around the first century AD, excavated at Daho-ri in Changwon, is the earliest item. The basket was found to contain scabbards, bows, ink brushes, lacquered boxes and folding fans. Bamboo baskets from the Goryeo Period have only been found in shipwrecks. They were used to hold utensils and food on a ship; their shapes and manufacturing methods are surprisingly similar to those produced in modern times.

## Net Bags from Mado Shipwreck No. 3

Net bags have an end at the bottom for slinging them over the shoulder, suggesting they were portable containers.

## *Jorak* from Mado Shipwreck No. 2

A *jorak* is a morning glory-shaped basket fitted with legs so it can be stood on the ground. It is very similar to the modern *jorak* used mainly in Jeollanam-do Province. On Jeju Island such baskets are known as *joreok*, *joragi* and *joregi*; and are used for carrying fish or seaweed over the shoulder. Peddlers would often carry a bunch of twenty such *jorak* when on their wanderings.

## Fabric Cover from Mado Shipwreck No. 3

This piece of hemp fabric has a knob at the center. Hemp is one of the most durable plant fibers due to its stability and strength, and contains few impurities. Its precise use is unknown, but it appears to have served as a cover of some kind.

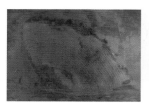  

## Wooden Combs and Fine-toothed Bamboo Combs from Mado Shipwreck No. 1

Most shipwrecks investigated in Korea have yielded wooden combs and fine-toothed bamboo combs. Sailors probably used them to trim their hair or catch lice during the long voyages.

## Top-knot Pins Salvaged from Myeongnyangdaecheop-ro Sea in Jindo

This is a top-knot hairpin(*donggot*) worn by a man. None has been found in shipwrecks so far, but several items made of bronze and silver have been salvaged from the seabed near Mado and Jindo Islands.

## Patch for Stopping up a Hole in a Stoneware Jar from Mado Shipwreck No. 3

This broken jar was mended by covering a hole with a patch.

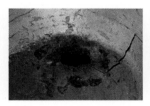 

# Chapter 9

# Korean Porcelains Recovered from Shipwrecks

Chapter 9

# Korean Porcelains Recovered from Shipwrecks

*"The Blue Color of Goryeo, the Best in the World*(高麗秘色天下
第一)*"*(*Xiuzhongjin*(袖中錦))

According to *Xiuzhongjin*, a book published during
the Song Dynasty, the Chinese nobility of this period sought
masterpieces from around the world, including Goryeo celadon.
Chinese celadon began to be produced in the third century AD
and enjoyed its golden age in the ninth and tenth centuries.
During this period, the royal family and nobles of the Goryeo
Dynasty imported celadon vessels from China. However, Goryeo
artisans began to produce celadon from the tenth century, and
in the eleventh century the kilns in Yongun-ri in Gangjin and

Yonggye-ri in Gochang fired high quality celadon wares. The twelfth century saw the golden age of Goryeo celadon, renowned for its jade green color, and various types of vessels began to appear.

In addition to Goryeo celadon, white porcelain of the Joseon Period is one of the most representative art forms of Korea because it embodies the simple and pure-white beauty associated with Koreans. Ceramic vessels account for the majority of artifacts salvaged from underwater excavations, and has thus been the subject of active studies.

While porcelain vessels excavated from inland sites provide information on the locations of the production sites, as well as firing methods and dates. In particular, the stratigraphy of kilns

Celadon Vesseles from of the Taean Shipwreck

laid with fragments of defective porcelain vessels shows the chronological variations in porcelain styles. Porcelain vessels salvaged from underwater excavations, however, show their process of circulation from producers to consumers. Moreover, as most vessels salvaged from the seafloor were unused items covered with mud and silt, they were generally well preserved objects. In addition to the ceramic vessels loaded as cargo on the ships, vessels used by sailors have also been frequently discovered. Celadon carriers such as the Sipidongpado and Taean Shipwrecks were fully loaded with celadon vessels. In particular, the Taean Shipwreck contained five neatly stacked layers of celadon that clearly show the packing method used to ship Goryeo celadon. Although Mado Shipwreck Nos. 1 and 2 were grain carriers, they also contained cargos of neatly packed celadon vessels, including lidded cups, bowls and dishes, as well as high-quality vessels such as prunus vases and gourd-shaped ewers. However, Mado Shipwreck No. 3 only contained about twenty celadon vessels used

**Batches of the Celadon Vessels from the Yamido Underwater Site**
No parts of the hull were identified.
**Celadon Vessels from Mado Shipwreck No. 3**
These vessels were found with bronze spoons and utensils.

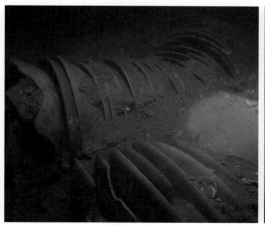
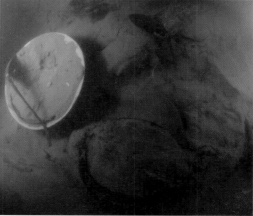

by the crew.

Meanwhile, the underwater excavations at the Doripo site in Muan and the Biando and Yamido Islands sites in Gunsan did not yield sunken hulls, but lots of porcelains vessels were salvaged from them. It seems that they were projected into the sea as cargo vessels were sinking.

## How Were Porcelain Vessels Transported?

Everyone knows that porcelain vessels are fragile objects. In order to load porcelain vessels on a ship, they had to be packed securely. In addition, shock-absorbent packing materials were inserted between the packs in order to transport them easily and prevent damages. The packing methods varied depending on the style of the porcelain, and the period and origin of the ships. In the case

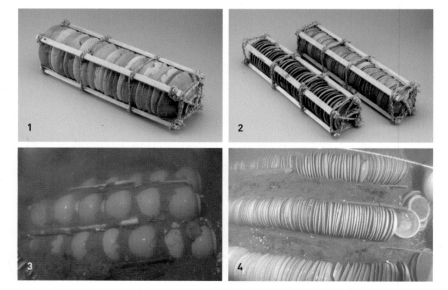

1, 2 Reconstruction of the Methods of Packing Celadon Bowls(1) and Dishes(2)

3, 4 Packing of Small Celadon Jars(3) and Dishes(4) from the Taean Shipwreck

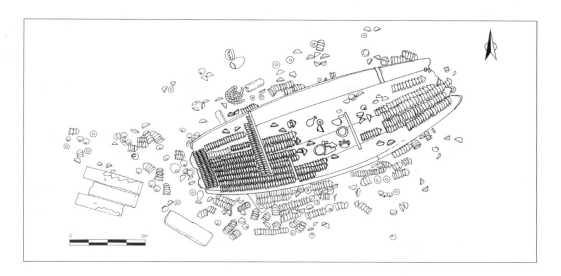

of Goryeo ships, batches of celadon bowls and dishes were stacked up one on top of the other. A wooden stick with grooves was placed on the uppermost vessel to secure the batches of celadon, and each batch was bound by straw ropes. Each batch contained 30-40 celadon bowls and 50-60 dishes respectively. Small jars and

**Illustration of the Sipidongpado Shipwreck**
Batches of celadon vessels were loaded in the bow and stern of the ship.

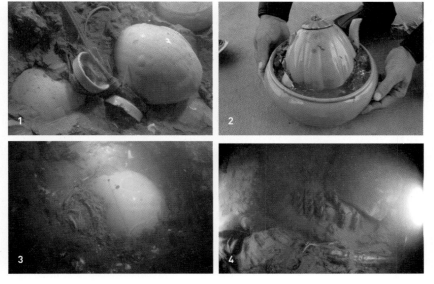

1 Packlig of a Celadon Oil Bottles from Taean Shipwreck

2 Packing of an Melon-shaped Celadon Ewer from the Taean Shipwreck

3 Packing of a Prunus Vase from Mado Shipwreck No. 2

4 Packing of Stoneware Jar from Mado Shipwreck No. 3
Jar containing a wooden tablet recording "Shipment of fish oil"

*Buncheong* Ware Vessels Found in a Net Bag from Mado Shipwreck No. 4

lidded cups were packed in the same way as bowls and dishes; but a rounded stick was used. In the case of celadon oil bottles, a wooden stick was placed between two bottles; and the necks of two bottles were bound with reeds.

However, it was impossible to prevent damage to vessels packed on ships that were frequently buffeted about on stormy seas. Therefore, the crew first laid a layer of straw or reeds on the bottom of the hull, and then placed batches of celadon vessels horizontally on that layer, repeating the process for several layers.

In addition to the dishes and oil bottles, special items such as ewers and prunus vases were individually packed. A celadon melon-shaped ewer was found inside a celadon jar. In order to prevent damage to it, straw was used as a shock-absorbent packing material. Likewise, a prunus vase containing sesame oil from Mado Shipwreck No. 2 was wrapped with straw, while a stoneware jar containing fish oil from Mado Shipwreck No.

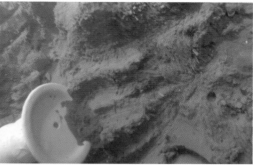

Batches of White Porcelains Found near Mado Shipwreck No. 4, and a Bag Packing White Porcelains

3 was wrapped with straw rope. It seems that these two vessels were more carefully packed than the others, perhaps because they contained liquid.

Only the *buncheong* vessels from Mado Shipwreck No. 4, a grain carrier, and the batches of white porcelains found near the hull of Mado Shipwreck No. 4 provide examples of the method of packing used for ceramic vessels in the Joseon Period. *Buncheong* vessels were placed in net bags woven with kudzu vines and loaded in a cooking place at the center of the hull.

In general, underwater surveys and preliminary excavations have only yielded a couple of white porcelain wares. However, a total of 111 packed white porcelain vessels were found on the seafloor near Mado Shipwreck No. 4. Although these were not found inside the hull, the method of packing them could be identified. As with celadon and *buncheong* vessels, the white porcelains were piled one on the top of the other, but they were packed with grain bag-shaped packing materials.

The following method of packing porcelain during the Yuan Dynasty was identified in the Shinan Shipwreck: porcelain

vessels were found stacked in layers inside circular and square-shaped wooden boxes, each of which was marked with Chinese characters indicating the identities of the recipients and owners of the vessels, along with various symbols. In order to prevent the porcelain vessels from rolling about, they were fixed by pieces of rosewood.

The porcelain vessels found in the Shinan Shipwreck were safely packed because this ship was an international merchant vessel dispatched on a long and potentially perilous voyage. One of the notable things about this ship's cargo is that some of boxes did not contain vessels produced in a single kiln. Various types of vessels produced at several klins in China were contained in a box to meet the buyer's demand.

## 12th-Century Goryeo Celadon Recovered from the Celadon Cargo Vessels

The heyday of Goryeo celadon occurred in the twelfth and thirteenth centuries, when diverse types of celadon vessels were mass produced in kilns in Gangjin and Buan, and then transported to Gaegyeong via the coastal route. As such, the Goryeo Shipwrecks identified so far contained celadon vessels produced in Jeolla-do Province.

Of the salvaged Goryeo ships, the Taean, Sipidongpado and Wando shipwrecks sunk in the twelfth century, with the latter two containing low-grade celadon wares that had been fired only once. Their quality was lower than the jade green celadon vessels produced in Gangjin, which were fired twice.

The Sipidongpado Shipwreck yielded diverse types of celadon vessels including flower-shaped dishes, oil bottles, small jars, vases with dish-shaped mouth, and flattened bottles. On the basis of typological studies of the celadon vessels yielded from this ship, it has been assumed that the Sipidongpado Shipwreck was carrying

Porcelain
Vessels from the
Sipidongpado
Shipwreck

products from the kiln in Sindeok-ri, Haenam.

The Wando Shipwreck yielded more than 30,000 celadon vessels including dishes, bowls, prunus vases and hourglass-shaped drums. Unlike the celadon vessels found in the Sipidongpado Shipwreck, some of the celadon vessels salvaged from the Wando Shipwreck are decorated with designs in underglaze iron. In fact, these celadon vessels with designs in underglaze iron—including prunus vases and hourglass-shaped drums—were clearly special high-grade products, as the clay used by potters to shape these vessels was finer than that used for making everyday items such as bowls and dishes. The production of vessels with designs in underglaze iron increased dramatically from the late eleventh to early twelfth century. The Wando ship was carrying celadon fired

Flower-shaped Dishes from the Sipidongpado Shipwreck(Upper) and the Sindeok-ri Kiln Site in Haenam(Lower)

Celadon Hourglass-shaped Drum with Underglaze Iron Design from Wando Shipwreck(Left), and Fragments of an Hourglass-shaped Drum from the Jinsan-ri Site(Right)

at the kiln in Jinsan-ri, Haenam, which was the main production center of such items.

The hourglass-shaped drum with underglaze iron design is the representative artifact of the Wando Shipwreck. This type of item, which was produced continuously at several celadon kiln sites, is assumed to have a ritual instrument used in the performance of rites by the royal family and temples.

As regards prunus vases, they began to be produced later than vases with a dish-shaped mouth, a number of which were recovered from the Sipidongpado Shipwreck, though no prunus vases

Vases with Dish-shaped Mouth Celadon Prunus Vases with Designs in Underglaze Iron from the Wando Shipwreck(Left) and Vase with Dish-shaped Mouth from the Sipidongpado Shipwreck(Right)

were found. This is definite evidence that the celadon vessels on the Wando Ship, which date to the middle-late twelfth century, were produced later than the objects found in the Sipidongpado Shipwreck, which were fired in the early twelfth century.

The Taean Shipwreck was a cargo vessel loaded with more than 25,000 celadon vessels. It is also the first Goryeo Shipwreck on which wooden tablets containing information on the production sites of the shipment of celadon vessels(Gangjin) have been found, and furnishes evidence of the date the ship sank(1131). Unlike the Sipidongpado and Wando Shipwrecks, which yielded low-grade celadon vessels, the Taean ship contained jade green celadon vessels.

Of the 188 kiln sites identified in Gangjin to date, 75 kilns belong to the Yongun-ri site. The celadon vessels salvaged from the Taean ship display similar typological characteristics and glaze to those discovered in Layer II of Yongun-ri Kiln No. 10, and are generally medium- and high-grade items. It might not have been easy to produce such large quantities of vessels in a kiln; therefore, it seems that the ship was loaded with vessels fired in several kilns in the Yongun-ri area.

In addition to daily utensils such as dishes, bowls and oil bottles, the ship yielded a number of special items including incense burners, ink-stones and *balu*(i.e. bowls used by Buddhists in temples). Fifty-one sets of *balu*(i.e. around 150 bowls, given that each set consisted of three or four bowls) were salvaged from the Taean Shipwreck. As the bottom of a *balu* is rounded, without foot that symbolizes

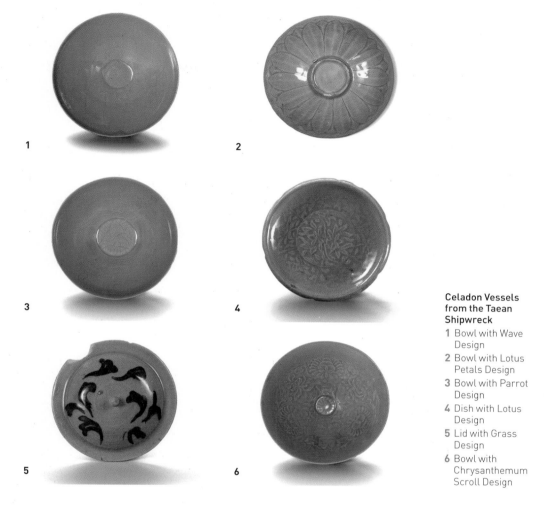

1

2

3

4

5

6

Celadon Vessels
from the Taean
Shipwreck
1 Bowl with Wave
   Design
2 Bowl with Lotus
   Petals Design
3 Bowl with Parrot
   Design
4 Dish with Lotus
   Design
5 Lid with Grass
   Design
6 Bowl with
   Chrysanthemum
   Scroll Design

mandala, they were stacked on straw or supporters, and straw was inserted into the gaps between them to absorb shocks.

In the twelfth century, Goryeo celadon entered its golden age. During this period, it was called jade green celadon; and various types of vessels began to appear. Hieroglyphic celadon wares decorated either partially or entirely with various motifs inspired by animals and plants are representative objects of the period.

**Celadon Vessels from the Yongun-ri Kiln Site in Gangjin**

1 Bowl with Wave Design
2 Bowl with Lotus Petals Design
3 Bowl with Parrot Design
4 Dish with Lotus Design
5 Lid with Grass Design
6 Bowl with Chrysanthemum Scroll Design

1

2

3

4

5

6

Notably, the most advanced production techniques of the time were required to produce them. Most of the extant hieroglyphic celadon vessels are inherited items, which makes it difficult to study their production dates and sites.

The toad-shaped ink-stone with paste-on-paste design and the lion-shaped incense burner recovered from the Taean ship are invaluable objects for establishing the chronological sequence of

*Balu* from the
Taean Shipwreck

hieroglyphic celadon vessels of Goryeo. The former is the only remaining object of its kind. Its surface is not a perfect jade-green, but it was produced with advanced techniques such as iron underglaze and slip decoration methods. It is also decorated with incised eggs design on the toad's back.

Unlike previous ones, the lion-shaped incense burner from Taean ship shows the unique artistic sensibility of the Goryeo

Celadon
Toad-shaped
Ink-stone with
Paste on Paste
Design
(Treasure No.
1782) from the
Taean Shipwreck

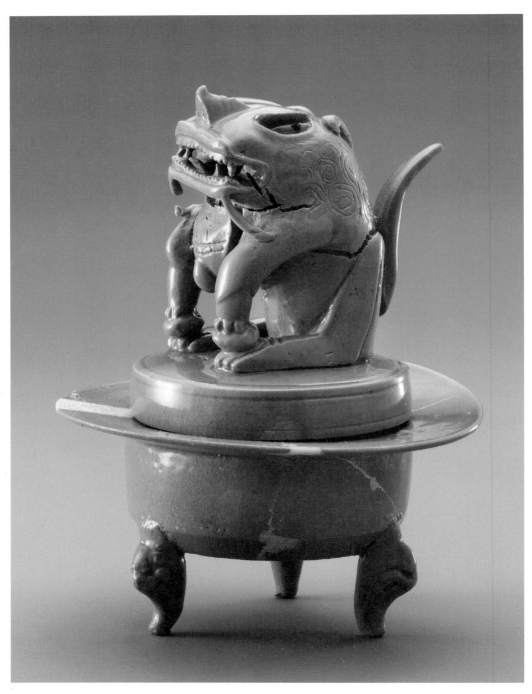

Celadon Lion-shaped Incense Burner

people with its humorous face. In Goryeo period, Lion was called *sanye*(狻猊) and considered as an animal with a penchant for fire and smoke. Therefore, it was one of the main motifs for incense burners.

In *Xuanhe Fengshi Gaoli Tujing*(宣和奉使高麗圖經)(a travelogue), Xu Jing describes the lion-shaped incense burner as follows:

> The lion-shaped incense burner is also jade green color. An crouched lion put on lotus flower-shaped stereobate. Of various objects, this is the best item...

## 13th-Century Goryeo Celadon Vessels Discovered off the Sea around Mado Island

Despite the confused political situation under the military regime and frequent attacks by Mongol troops, Goryeo art reached its zenith in the thirteenth century with the production of inlaid celadon vessels; and, from the late thirteenth century onward, various types of vessels with new designs quite unlike the previous jade green and inlaid celadon vessels began to be produced while Goryeo was under the sway of the Yuan Dynasty.

Mado Shipwreck Nos. 1 and 2, which were excavated in 2009 and 2010, respectively, contained celadon vessels produced around this time. As these two ships were not celadon carriers like the Wando and Taean Shipwrecks, but grain carriers, fewer porcelain vessels were found on these ships than on the celadon containers, although they yielded hundreds of celadon vessels shipped as cargo. Moreover, the wooden tablets yielded from both shipwrecks indicate the date of the shipwrecks(i.e. 1208 for Mado Shipwreck No. 1 and before 1213 for Mado Shipwreck No. 2), thus enabling researchers to establish the chronology of Goryeo celadon.

Most of the vessels salvaged from these two wrecks are bowls, dishes and cups. Except for several undecorated vessels and bowls with a parrot design, most are decorated with a lotus petals design. In addition, both shipwrecks contained top-shaped cups and lidded cups which, along with the aforementioned lotus petals and parrot designs, are the most representative types of vessels and decorative designs of Goryeo celadon of the mid-Goryeo

Celadon Vessels
from Mado
Shipwreck No. 1
1 Bowl with
   Incised Parrot
   Design
2 Lidded Cup
3 Bowl with Lotus
   petals Design
4 Cup

Period(i.e. from the late eleventh to the middle of the thirteenth century). These are generally classified as Gangjin-type wares, named after the Yongun-ri kiln site in Gangjin, the main production center of Goryeo celadon, although other kilns also produced Gangjin-type vessels during this period.

Before the excavation of Mado Shipwreck No. 1, researchers claimed that such types of vessels were produced in the eleventh and twelfth centuries. However, the celadon vessels with a design in underglaze iron and low-grade celadon vessels loaded on this ship suggest that these types were even produced in the thirteenth century. Therefore, the excavation of Mado Shipwreck No. 1 presented an opportunity to shed new light on the chronology of Goryeo celadon in the middle period.

These two shipwrecks contained celadon vessels with inlaid designs. Inlay is the decorative technique by which reddish or white

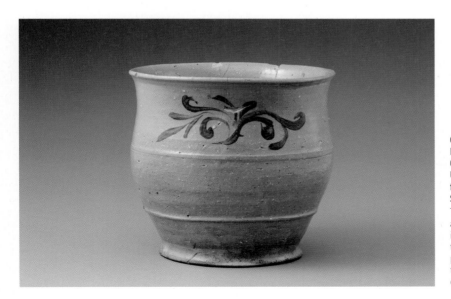

**Celadon Flowerpot with Grass Design in Underglaze Iron from Mado Shipwreck No. 1**
This is regarded as an important item for revealing the date when the production of this type of vessel was discontinued.

Celadon Gourd-shaped Ewer with Inlaid Peony and Lotus Design

clay is inserted into a pattern or design stamped on the surface of a vessel by a seal and carved with a burin before glazing. A few inlaid celadon vessels produced in the early Goryeo Period have been discovered so far; it appears that this type of vessel was produced in large quantities from the twelfth century.

Before the excavation of Mado Shipwrecks Nos. 1 and 2, a few inlaid celadon vessels looted from the royal tombs of Goryeo were the only materials available to researchers attempting to establish a chronology.

A number of vessels recovered from Mado Shipwreck Nos. 1 and 2 including an inlaid celadon ewer and an inlaid celadon prunus vase, proved that inlaid celadon began to be produced on a large scale before 1208. These vessels are also important materials for establishing the chronology of Goryeo inlaid celadon.

A ewer from Mado Shipwreck No. 1 is a gourd-shaped vessel inlaid with peony blossom and lotus flower designs. It has a circular ring for connecting the lid and the handle with a string. It was found together with a saucer, which was used for containing warm water for conserving the temperature of the liquid contained by the ewer.

A wooden tablet attached to a celadon prunus vase uncovered from Mado Shipwreck No. 2 reveals that the vase contained sesame oil. An anarudda design is inlaid on its shoulder; its body is inlaid with chrysanthemum, peony blossom, bamboo, reed, willow tree, and *Hibiscus esculentus L* designs; and its bottom is inlaid with lotus petals and lighting designs.

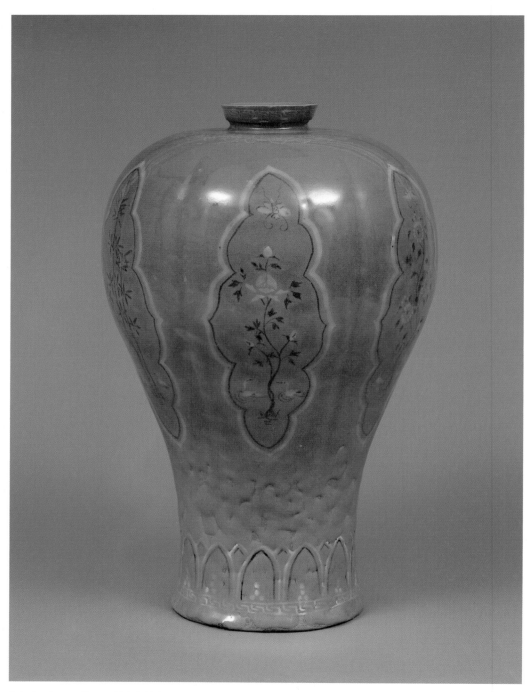

Celadon Prunus Vase with Inlaid Chrysanthemum, Peony, Willow, Heron, and Bamboo Designs(Treasure No. 1783)

## 14th-Century Goryeo Celadon Vessels Discovered at Doripo in Muan

Celadon vessels marked with the year of the sexagenary cycle and prunus vases with the title of the government offices that ordered them are the representative celadon vessels of the late Goryeo Period, i.e. the fourteenth century. At that time, the political situation in Goryeo was very chaotic, and was characterized by King Gongmin's reforms, the emergence of powerful scholar-officials, incursions by Japanese raiders, and the transition from the Yuan to the Ming Dynasty in China. In this period, the celadon industry in Gangjin collapsed, and the quality of Goryeo celadon deteriorated due to the use of poor-quality paste and glaze. The 638 Goryeo celadon vessels recovered from Doripo in Muan explicitly attest to these circumstances.

The inlaid celadon vessels found at this site were the product of Kiln No. 10 of the Sadang-ri Kiln in Gangjin, and appear to be wares paid as tax-in-kind to the royal family and government

Celadon Vessels with Inlaid Design from the Doripo Site in Muan(Left), Celadon Vessels from Kiln No. 10 at Sadang-ri, Gangjin(Right)

offices. It is possible that they were thrown into the sea when a celadon container either ran into a storm or was looted by Japanese raiders. These vessels are characterized by more a thicker wall and a browner glaze than earlier inlaid celadon. Their body is stamped with simplified cloud, chrysanthemum and lotus flower. Goryeo inlaid celadon produced in the fourteenth century influenced the types and designs of inlaid celadon and *buncheong* wares produced in the early Joseon Period.

## 'Buncheong' Ware Vessels, Tax-in-kind of the Joseon Period(15th Century) Found on Mado Shipwreck No. 4

The *buncheong* wares recovered from Mado Shipwreck No. 4 appear to have been produced near Naju, Jeolla-do Province, and are typical porcelain vessels paid as tax-in-kind in the early Joseon Period. Vessels paid as tax-in kind is the porcelain that was produced as the same size and design with the sample sent from the central government. The *buncheong* ware vessel with densely clustered stamped patterns is the representative case. Three vessels are incised with the Chinese characters *naeseom*(內贍), the name of goverment office. According to *Joseonwangjo silrok*(朝鮮王朝實錄)(Annals of the Joseon Dynasty), the king ordered in 1417 that the porcelain vessels paid as tax-in-kind be incised with the title of the office, which suggests that they were produced in the early fifteenth century.

Following the decline of inlaid celadon in the fourteenth century,

*Buncheong* Ware Vessels from Mado Shipwreck No. 4

it was replaced by *buncheong* ware in the early fifteenth century, when the throne of the Joseon Dynasty stabilized. Of the various types of porcelain vessels produced in Korea, *buncheong* is the most simplified and folk-like, reaching its peak in the reign of King Sejong. As a *bunwon*(分院), government-run kiln firing white porcelains, was built in Gwangju, Gyeonggi-do Province, in 1467-1469, the production of *buncheong* wares decreased dramatically and came to be produced in small-scale kilns, before finally being discontinued in the early sixteenth century.

## 19th-Century White Porcelains Recovered from the Sea around Mado Island

Before the discovery of Mado Shipwreck No. 4, a batch of white porcelains consisting of fifty-nine bowls, thirty dishes, twenty cups and two candlesticks was salvaged from the Sea around Mado Island in 2014. It appears that white porcelains produced at the *Bunwon* in Gwangju were mainly transported to Seoul via the Hangang River in the Joseon Period; no evidence has been found to suggest that they were ever transported by the sea route, and it had been acknowledged that white porcelain wares were not transported over long distances since their production sites were situated close to the main consumption sites. However, a batch of white porcelains recovered from the Sea around Mado Island contradicted this view and proved that such vessels were sometimes transported via sea.

Therefore, the batch of porcelains found in the sea near Mado has attracted scholars' attention. These low-grade white porcelain wares seem to have been produced at kilns in Chungcheong-do Province in the late eighteenth or early nineteenth century

**White Porcelains from the Sea around Mado Island**
Two candlesticks can be seen each end of the photo.

when the production and circulation of porcelain vessels in the provinces developed dramatically. Since a ship's hull and other artifacts were not found together with these vessels, it is not clear how they ended up there.

Two candlesticks are among the most notable items salvaged on this occasion, and reflect the circumstances of the time. Candles made of wax were considered precious items in the Joseon Period, and were thus used at the royal court or at the weddings ceremony. As the government prohibited the use of candles in the early Joseon Period, people used torches made of resin or oil lamps. With the introduction of the culture of the Qing Dynasty in Korea in the late Joseon Period, an appreciation of fine things, such as antiques and gardening, spread among scholars. Candles, as a luxury item, were disseminated to the people.

## ● Revelation of Porcelain Production Techniques and Sites by Scientific Analysis ●

Porcelain vessels salvaged from underwater sites arouse our curiosity about when, where and how they were produced. Although the contents of wooden tablets yielded from shipwrecks can provide answers to such questions, more accurate answers can be found through scientific analysis.

In order to seek answers concerning the production techniques of porcelain, the patterns of minerals contained in glaze and body have to be identified first. The body is a mixture of kaolin and additives, such as quartz, feldspar and mica. Such minerals can be observed through polarizing and electron microscopes.

Using polarized light microscopy, it is possible to determine type of mineral by passing polarized light through the polished thin porcelain pieces. Researchers observe the types and sizes of the minerals undergoing analysis, and measure the types of additives they contain and their melting rates. Data collected from polarized light microscopy are used as basic materials in a detailed analysis. For example, if the size of the feldspar particles is abnormally large, the vessel must have been fired at a low temperature; and if the hexagonal-shaped quartz crystals are abnormally large or have an unusual shape, then the vessel was produced using the wrong technique.

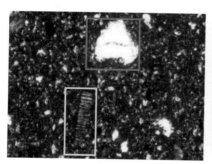 

**Polarized Microscope Images of a Well-fired Shard of Porcelain(Left) and a Pooly-fired Shard of Porcelain(Right)**

Various types of minerals can be observed here. The particles in the red, yellow and blue squares are quartz, feldspar and mica, respectively. Poorly-fired shard of porcelain[Right] has mica and angular quartz, which means it was fired at a lower temperature than well-fired shard of porcelain(Left).

During the porcelain firing process, minerals are melted and re-crystallized. If a vessel is not fired at the correct temperature level, particles of quartz and feldspar remain on its surface. By using a Scanning Electron Microscope(SEM), the types and patterns of the minerals, and the thickness and particle of the glaze are more accurately discerned. Electrons interact with atoms in the shards of porcelain, producing various signals that contain information about a sample's composition. The composition of porcelain can be detected in a Backscattered Electron Image, which marks the atoms of minerals by different degrees of brightness, but does not show the color of the minerals.

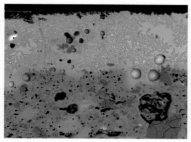

**Scanning Electron Microscope Images of a well-fired Shard of Porcelain(Left) and a Poorly-fired Shard of Porcelain(Right)**
As this vessel(Right) was not fired at an adequate temperature, particles of quartz and feldspar remain.

X-Ray Diffraction Analysis(XRD) is another scientific method of determining the composition of porcelain. Whereas researchers can directly observe minerals formed in the past with the naked eye, XRD is a method of identifying the atomic and molecular structure of a crystal, in which the crystalline atoms cause a beam of incident X-rays to diffract into many specific directions. By measuring the angles and intensities of these diffracted beams reflected from samples(porcelains), researchers can determine the compositions of porcelain vessels.

If mullite(also known as porcelainite) is detected in a sample through X-Ray Diffraction Analysis, the firing temperature of that porcelain vessel must have been above 1,100℃, because this mineral is produced by the oxidization and decomposition of kaolin when heated above 1,000℃.

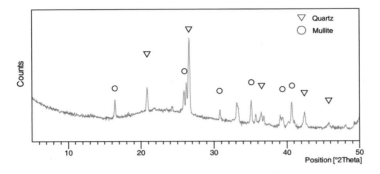

**Result of X-Ray Diffraction Analysis of a Porcelain Sample**
This graph shows that it contains quartz and mullite, but does not contain
kaolin or feldspar. It is assumed to have been fired at over 1,000℃.

After revealing the production techniques and firing temperatures of porcelain vessels
by microscopy and XRD, researchers conduct elementary and microelement analyses.
The main elements composing the body are Si, Al, Fe, Ca, Na, K, Mg, Ti, Mn, and P. In
order to measure the quantity of these elements, researchers use X-ray Fluorescence
Spectroscopy(XRF), which involves the emission of characteristic "secondary"(or
fluorescent) X-ray from a material that has been excited by bombarding it with high-energy
X-rays or gamma rays. The amount of X-ray fluorescence in each atom differs according
to the amount of each mineral contained in the body. By measuring the pattern of X-ray
fluorescence, researchers can detect the types and quantities of minerals in a porcelain
vessel.

Meanwhile, Inductively Coupled Plasma Atomic Emission Spectrometry(ICP-AES) is a
method of measuring the types and quantities of microelements constituting the body
of a vessel. It is a type of emission spectroscopy that uses inductively coupled plasma
to produce excited atoms and ions that emit electromagnetic radiation at wavelengths
characteristic of a particular element.

On the basis of a body that contains particular elements, the provenance of ceramic
vessels salvaged from shipwrecks can be detected by comparing the particular elements
contained in them with those of vessels recovered from kiln sites. For example, the Taean
Shipwreck yielded more than 25,000 celadon vessels. Working on the hypothesis that

these celadon vessels might have been produced at kilns in Gangjin on the basis of the information contained on the wooden tablets recovered from the ship, the research team conducted a study on their provenance by comparing the elements of samples from the Taean Shipwreck with those collected from Kiln No. 16 at Yongun-ri, Kiln Nos. 9 and 10 at Sadang-ri, Kiln No. 23 at Gyeyul-ri in Gangjin, and kilns at Jinsan-ri and Sindeok-ri in Haenam, and at Yucheon-ri and Jinseo-ri in Buan. The results of these analyses show that the elements of celadon salvaged from the Taean Shipwreck are similar to those found in Gangjin, but differ from those found in Buan and Haenam. Given that the results of these analyses correspond with the contents of the wooden tablets, the research team finally concluded that the celadon vessels loaded on the Taean Shipwreck were produced at kilns in Gangjin.

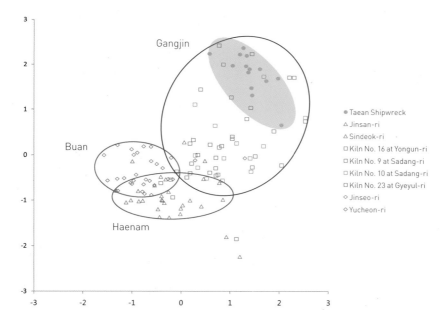

**Graph of the Celadon Production Sites Contained in the Taean Shipwreck**

# Chapter 10

# Conservation and Measurement of Dates of Shipwrecks

# Conservation and Measurement of Dates of Shipwrecks

At first glance, the remaining wooden hulls of the sunken ships found in the sea and mudflats appear to be relatively well preserved. However, when we press the tissue of the wooden material with a finger, it becomes clear that it is very degraded, almost like a sponge. Wooden materials that have been only swollen water for a long time have no such weak tissues. If that is the case, what is it that makes the tissue of wooden shipwrecks so soft? In fact, the culprits are the microscopic life forms that are not visible to the human eye.

After sinking, wooden ships gradually become damaged, and their hull structures are scattered by sea and tidal currents. The

The Hull of the
Anjwa Shipwreck
Showing Signs of
Damage by Marine
Borers(Left)
Calcified Remains
of Shipworms
(Right)

remaining hull also loses its original shape due to the depredations of marine borers including shipworms(the genus Teredo and Pholad) and gribbles(the genus Limnonia), which destroy wood by boring into and eating it.

When shipworms initially penetrate into the tissue, they bore small holes of about 1 mm in diameter. However, as they grow, the holes become larger, expanding to about 7-10 mm in diameter. Once they penetrate into tissue, they spend rest of their life in there. They not only bore and eat away the outer surface, but also penetrate the interior of a wooden material; and even cover with lime the surface of the tunnels that they bore. In sum, they cause severe damage to the hull of a sunken ship.

However, the mud and silt that cover a sunken hull prevent

Remains of a Hull
Buried under a
Mudflat
Parts of a wooden
hull buried in
deep mud were
relatively well
preserved.
(Left), Cell Walls
Decomposed
by Soft-Rot
Fungi(Right)

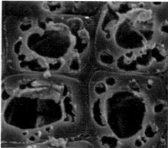

# ● Conservation of Waterlogged Archaeological Wood ●

Hulls are discovered submerged in wet environments such as seas, rivers and lakes. Wooden materials excavated from underwater sites are called "waterlogged archaeological wood," which, in other words, refers to wooden objects that are filled with water in the spaces where their cellulose, hemicelluloses and lignin have decomposed. When a waterlogged archaeological wood is exposed to the air, its original form is changed by the rapid evaporation of its water content.

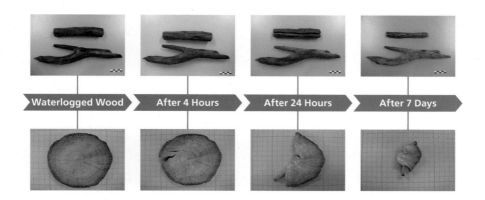

For example, the conservation team of the institute conducted an experiment to examine the change of moisture content of a water-saturated oak tree found in Mado Shipwreck No. 3, which sank 800 years ago. Its maximum moisture content was found to be 583 percent. After exposing it to air for four hours, the wood began to crack. After one day, it shrank in size by three fifths compared to its original form. After one week, its form had changed dramatically due to the evaporation of the moisture contained in its tissue.

Maximum moisture content is the quantity of water contained in a given material, such as soil, rock, ceramics, fruit or wood. In general, the water content of a living tree is about 100 percent. Therefore, a piece of waterlogged archaeological wood whose maximum moisture content is 583 percent will retain its original shape very well, but this is because it contains 5.8 times more water than a living tree. Therefore, in order to maintain excavated waterlogged archaeological wood items in their original form and preserve them safely, they should be stored in a water-saturated state.

attacks by marine borers by blocking oxygen from getting into the hull. Nevertheless, sunken hulls covered by mud and silt are not entirely safe from destruction, as soft-rot fungi that eat waterlogged archaeological wood, and erosion and tunneling bacteria living amid the oxygen-free environment also attack it. An organ attacked by them may keep its form, but its physical and chemical characteristics will change as an empty space is formed in the cell wall.

## Conservation of the Shinan Shipwreck

In Korea, it is no exaggeration to say that the development of conservation for waterlogged archaeological wood began and was finally completed with the project for the conservation of the Shinan Shipwreck. Before this project, the wooden boat excavated at Wolji Pond in Gyeongju was restored by a conservation treatment. However, a systematic process for the conservation treatment of waterlogged wooden materials was established during this project. Of the various types of waterlogged wooden materials, sunken hulls require the most complex conservation process. The full conservation of a shipwreck takes anywhere from fifteen to thirty years. For instance, the project to reconstruct the Shinan Shipwreck took twenty-three years, including nineteen years for the conservation(1981-1999) and eleven years for the reconstruction(1994-2004).

After salvaging the sunken hull and its constituent parts from the

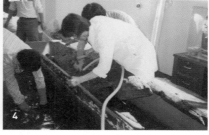

sea, preventing the evaporation of their moisture content was the most pressing task. These were wrapped carefully with non-woven fabrics or vinyl in the excavation field to prevent their surface from drying out, and then moved to the conservation laboratory. The institute's conservation laboratory began by carrying out the desalination of the hull and other parts. Any soluble salt in the wooden materials was removed by soaking them to tap water. During the desalination, the conservationists removed the mud, shells and marine borers attached to the surface and interior of the hull using brushes and bamboo knives.

Generally speaking, the desalination for shipwrecks requires more than three years. During this period, conservators try to find the best method of conservation for a hull by examining the species and the rate of decomposition of the wooden materials. Analyses of the hull of the Shinan Shipwreck showed that it was made of

*Pinus massoniana*, a species of pine tree; and that the maximum moisture content of the various parts of the hull varied from an average of 569 percent in the most severely decomposed parts to one of 202.9 percent in the weakly decomposed parts. In addition, the analyses showed that the wooden materials had been attacked by marine borers and bacteria.

After completing the desalination, the lab conducted a treatment designed to consolidate the hull. This method, which is also called a "hardening treatment," is the most time-consuming time part of the conservation of a shipwreck. In order to consolidate or harden the wooden materials, various chemicals and organic matters, such as polyethylene glycol(PEG), sugars, and alcohols are used. Of these, PEG is the most widely used chemical in the conservation of wooden hulls in the world. PEG comes in a variety of molecular weights, and ranges from viscous liquids(e.g. PEG 400) to hard waxes(e.g. PEG 4,000) at 40-45℃. After impregnating the lower weight PEG 400 into parts whose rate of decomposition

**Consolidation of Waterlogged Archaeological Wood Using PEG**
PEG impregnated into the decomposed cell walls reinforces the hardness of the wooden materials. (Hoffmann, ○ = Moisture, ● = PEG)

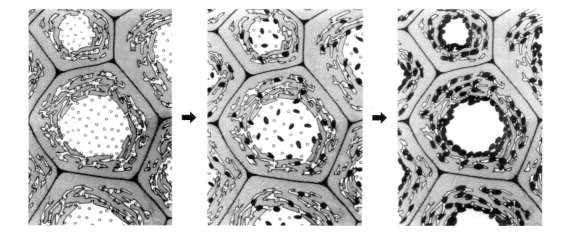

**Consolidation**
Conservators poring PEG 4,000 into the water tank containing water and parts of the hull(Left)
Removing PEG from the Surface of the Keel of the Shinan Shipwreck after Consolidation Treatment(Right)

is relatively low, the heavier PEG 400 is injected into the severely decomposed parts.

Consolidation is not the last procedure in the conservation of a shipwreck. After injecting chemicals and organic matters into the wooden materials; the probability of shrinkage of a wooden hull decreases dramatically, however, the air-drying process is essential to solidify and harden the liquids injected into the wooden materials and to slowly evaporate any moisture remaining in them. For this reason, the humidity of the room in which the hull is being treated is gradually reduced.

The Shinan Ship was finally restored after completing the air-drying process of the hull. However, this is not the end of the conservation of shipwrecks. Control of the post-preservation environment is also of paramount importance. Even a hull that has been successfully restored by conservation will be damaged if kept in unsuitable conditions. Therefore, the International Council of Museums(ICOM) regulates the conservation condition of wooden materials, such as hulls, to a control temperature of

20±2℃, humidity of 50±5%, and light of 200lx. In order to keep the Shinan Ship under suitable conditions, the researchers at the institute check the temperature and humidity and observe the hull regularly.

Some wooden materials do not require consolidation, and directly proceed to the air-drying process. Rosewood, the finest type of wood loaded on the Shinan Shipwreck, is a representative case in this respect. The air-dried specific gravity of rosewood is 0.8-0.85. Specific gravity is the ratio of the density of a substance to the density of a reference substance; equivalently, it is the ratio of the mass of a substance to the mass of a reference substance for the

Reassembling the
Side Planks of the
Shinan Shipwreck

same given volume. The air-dried specific gravity of pine wood is 0.43. Therefore, the tissue of rosewood is about two times harder than that of pine wood. Hard woods such as rosewood are less prone, relatively speaking, to attack by bacteria and marine borers. The maximum moisture content of the rosewood recovered from the Shinan Shipwreck is 73.3 percent. Therefore, after completing the desalinization treatment, the institute gradually removed the moisture contained in the rosewood through several air-drying stages conducted over a long period of time. This case clearly shows that the conservationists conducted different conservation treatments on wooden materials in accordance with their conditions.

## Measurement of the Sunken Dates of Shipwrecks Dendrochronology

Establishing the date of a shipwreck is the most significant puzzle that researchers and investigators have to unravel. How do they solve this question? One might think that referring to historical sources is the easiest way to do this, but unfortunately very few historical documents contain any information about shipwrecks in Korea. Fortunately, the wooden cargo tags recovered from various shipwrecks often give significant clues to the dates on which the ships sank, while studies on the chronology of ceramic vessels salvaged from them provide significant data that make it possible to infer the dates of the shipwrecks. However, it is very difficult to postulate the date of a shipwreck that does not yield such artifacts.

Under these circumstances, the scientific approach is the important and reliable method of revealing the date of a shipwreck. The hulls of all ancient shipwrecks found in Korea are of course made of wood. As such, studies of the tree rings can determine the logging dates of the wood used to build these ships. Korea has four distinct seasons. Tree rings are the growth layers of wood, and are produced each year in the stems and roots of trees. In climates with well-defined alternations of the seasons(either cold and warm or wet and dry), wood cells produced when water is easily available and growth is rapid(generally corresponding to the spring or wet season) are often noticeably larger and have thinner walls than those produced later in the season when the supply of water has

Tree Ring Patterns(Wide or Narrow) Showing Unique Periodic Patterns

diminished and growth is slower. There is thus a sharp contrast between the small, thick-walled late-season wood cells produced one year, and the large, thin-walled cells of the spring wood of the following year.

Trees from the same region tend to develop the same patterns of ring width. Dendrochronology, or tree-ring dating, is a scientific method of dating based on the analysis of the patterns of tree rings, also known as growth rings. Dendrochronology can date the time at which tree rings were formed to the exact calendar year in diverse types of wood.

In order to apply the tree-ring dating method to a shipwreck, researchers first have to establish the tree-ring pattern of the wooden materials of the sunken hull. To extract core samples, they use an increment borer, a specialized tool that is used to extract a

Sampling of Tree Rings: Coring Method(Upper) Camera Photographing (Lower)

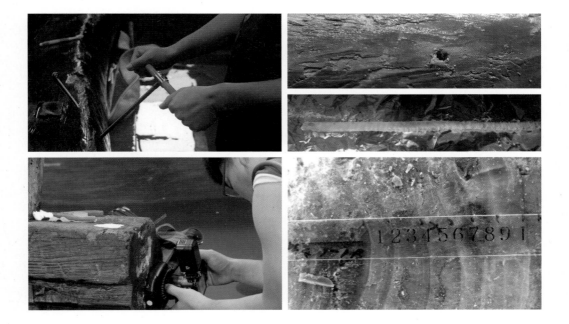

section of wood tissue from a tree with relatively minor damage to the plant itself. After smoothing the surface of the extracted core samples in order to observe the ring patterns clearly, researchers measure the width of the tree rings, which are usually 0.3 cm in diameter.

Establishing the sample chronology of a shipwreck is the first procedure. After taking photos of the tree rings of samples extracted from wooden materials, the photos are arranged in chronological order. The bark of the samples indicates the logging date of the trees. Researchers draw a sample chronology graph by matching the overlapping orders of tree rings of the same width by measuring them in units of 0.01 mm.

The construction date of a shipwreck can be calculated by matching the sample chronology of the shipwreck with the master chronology. This is called "cross-dating." In order to cross-date a sunken hull, it is essential to establish the master chronology of a species of tree used in a particular region.

Timber core samples are sampled and used to measure the width of annual growth rings. By taking samples from living trees and matching them with samples from different sites within a particular region, researchers can build a comprehensive historical sequence, in other words, the master chronology. The master chronology is either an average tree-ring chronology for a particular region, or one derived locally from a number of closely matching individual tree-ring chronologies. The master chronology forms the reference against which new ring series may be compared and dated. In the USA, Europe, South America and Japan, the maximum time spans of the master chronologies of certain species of trees, which are over 8,000 BP, were established. For example, the maximum time span of the chronologies of the European oak(*Quercus* spp.) and the Scots pine tree is about 12,400 BP.

In Korea, the master chronology of the pine tree(*Pinus densiflora* S. et Z) was first put together in November 1999. By measuring the overlapping pattern of tree-ring samples extracted from Geurakjeon Hall of Hwaamsa Temple in Wanju, Geunjeongjeon

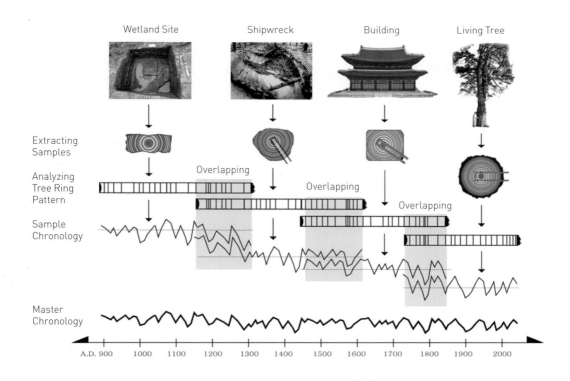

Establishment of the Master Chronology

Hall of Gyeongbokgung Palace, and Sungryemun Gate, the researchers built up an unbroken sequence extending from as far back as 1170 to the present day. However, the institute failed to match the sample chronology extracted from the sunken hulls with this master chronology.


## Radiocarbon Dating and Wiggle Matching

Radiocarbon dating is the most extensively used scientific method of determining the age of an artifact containing organic material in the field of archaeological research. During its lifespan, a plant or an animal exchanges carbon with its surroundings, so the carbon it contains will have the same proportion of $^{14}C$ as the atmosphere. Once it dies, it ceases to acquire $^{14}C$, but the $^{14}C$ within its biological material at that time will continue to decay, and so the ratio of $^{14}C$ to $^{12}C$ in its remains will gradually decrease. The half-life of $^{14}C$ is about 5,730 years. However, accurate measurement of the $^{14}C$ activity of samples is affected by fluctuations of the $^{14}C/^{12}C$ ratio in the atmosphere, background cosmic radiation, and changes in the earth's magnetic fields. Therefore, the radiocarbon dates measured in organic samples have to be calibrated. However, the calibration of radiocarbon dates has some limitations, because it is not easy to calibrate errors caused by changes in the earth's magnetic fields and the background solar magnetic field, called "wiggle."

Wiggle matching is a dating method that uses the non-linear

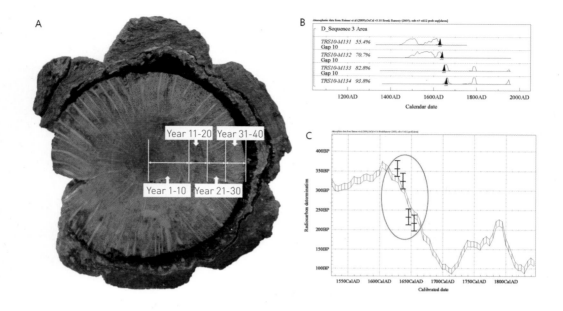

A

B
Atmospheric data from Reimer et al (2009);OxCal v3.10 Bronk Ramsey (2005); cub r:5 sd:12 prob usp[chron]

D_Sequence 3 Area

| TRS10-M131 | 55.4% |
| Gap 10 | |
| TRS10-M132 | 70.7% |
| Gap 10 | |
| TRS10-M133 | 82.8% |
| Gap 10 | |
| TRS10-M134 | 93.8% |

1200AD    1400AD    1600AD    1800AD    2000AD

Calendar date

C

Radiocarbon determination

400BP
350BP
300BP
250BP
200BP
150BP
100BP

1550CalAD   1600CalAD   1650CalAD   1700CalAD   1750CalAD   1800CalAD

Calibrated date

Year 11-20  Year 31-40
Year 1-10  Year 21-30

relationship between $^{14}$C age and calendar age obtained from dendrochronology. This approach can be employed most directly in the case of wood samples with many years of growth present where a tree-ring series of an unknown date can be compared against a similarly-constructed $^{14}$C calibration curve derived from wood whose age is known. The researcher first extracts 4-5 samples in accordance with the chronological order of each ring in a tree; and measures the radiocarbon dates of each sample. Although the radiocarbon date of each sample can show a wide margin of error, researchers can reduce the error range of radiocarbon dates to within 20-30 years by comparing the radiocarbon dates measured in each sample. Thus, the institute measured the dates of the Taean and Yeongheungdo Shipwrecks, and Mado Shipwrecks No. 3 and 4 by applying wiggle matching

Wiggle Matching
A: Extracting Core Samples
B: Radiocarbon Date of Each Sample
C: Graph Showing Wiggle Matching

Photo A shows a wooden post aged in 40 years that was unearthed from a site dating back to the Joseon Period. The radiocarbon date produced from a sample extracted in the last bark ranges from 1646 to 1955 AD. Therefore, the researchers conducted wiggle matching between the $^{14}$C age and the calendar age in order to match the shape of a series of closely, sequentially spaced $^{14}$C dates with the $^{14}$C calibration curve by extracting 4 samples set at 10-year intervals in each in accordance with the chronological order of each ring in the tree, and thereby revealed that it was logged between 1650 and 1655.

dating to their tree-ring sequences; and the results of the samples extracted from the hull of the Taean Shipwreck show the time range of 1126 to 1150 with 95.4 percent reliability. This result proves that the year of *sinhae*(辛亥) written on the wooden cargo tags recovered from the Taean Shipwreck is 1131.

# Maritime Museum in the Book

Underwater archaeology, in other words, the study of archaeological materials lying in seas, rivers and lakes, is a sub-discipline of archaeology. This is the chapter to introduce the representative artifacts salvaged from the underwater sites in Korea, porcelain vessels from the Shinan Shipwreck and celadon vessels from shipwrecks sunken in the Goryeo Period. This is our hope that the readers can feel the breath of the people who produced, shipped and used these objects.

# Goryeo Celadon Vessels

**Celadon Bowl with Incised Wave and Fish Design**
—
Goryeo, 12C
Taean, Taean Shipwreck
H. 4.7cm D. 15.4cm

**Celadon Flower-shaped Dish with
Incised Lotus Design**
—
Goryeo, 12C
Taean, Taean Shipwreck
H. 4.0cm D. 17.5cm

**Celadon Bowl with
Impressed Peony Design**

—

Goryeo, 12C
Taean, Taean Shipwreck
H. 6.1cm D. 18.5cm

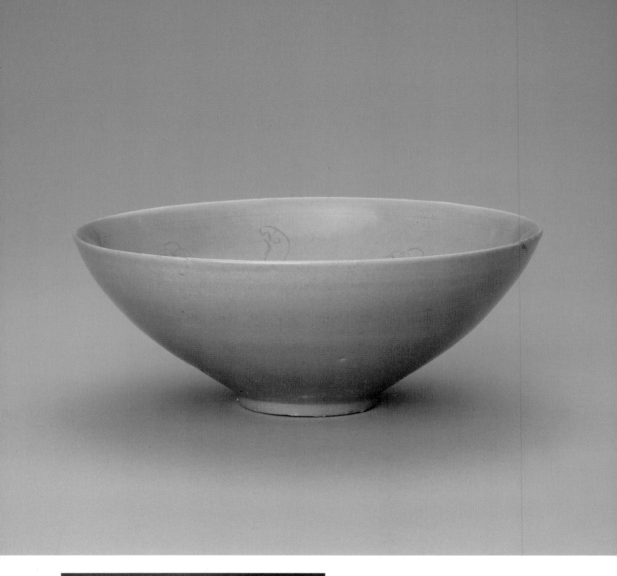

**Celadon Bowl with Incised Parrot Design**

—

Goryeo, 12C
Taean, Taean Shipwreck
H. 7.4cm D. 18.2cm

**Celadon Bowl with Carved Lotus Petals Design**
—
Goryeo, 12C
Taean, Taean Shipwreck
H. 8.5cm D. 16.2cm

**Celadon Lidded Case with
Incised Line Design**
—
Goryeo, 12C
Taean, Taean Shipwreck
H. 4.5cm D. 6.6cm

**Celadon Oil Bottle**
—
Goryeo, 12C
Taean, Taean Shipwreck
H. 5.2cm

**Celadon Melon-shaped Ewer**
—
Goryeo, 12C
Taean, Taean Shipwreck
H. 16.8cm

**Celadon Bowl with Inlaid Peony
Scroll and Phoenix Design**

—

Goryeo, 14C
Sea of Doripo in Muan
H. 9.2cm D. 16.5cm

**Celadon Bowl**
—
Goryeo, 12C
Gunsan, Sipidongpado Shipwreck
H. 7.8cm D. 18.2cm

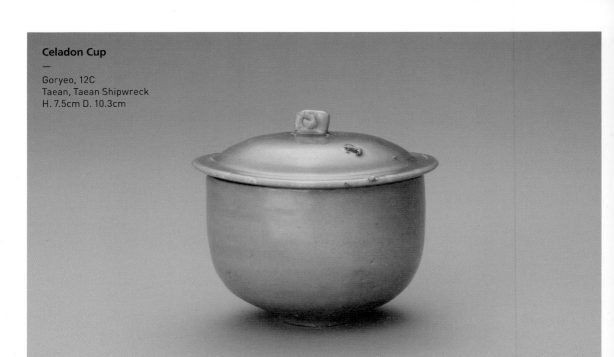

**Celadon Cup**
—
Goryeo, 12C
Taean, Taean Shipwreck
H. 7.5cm D. 10.3cm

**Celadon Cup with Incised
Chrysanthemums Design**
—
Goryeo, 12C
Sea of Myeongnyangdaecheop-ro in Jindo
H. 4.3cm D. 9.6cm

**Celadon Prunus Vase with
Incised Lotus Design**
—
Goryeo, 13C
Taean, Mado Shipwreck No.2
H. 39cm

**Celadon Dish with Impressed Peony Design**
—
Goryeo, 13C
Sea of Myeongnyangdaecheop-ro in Jindo
H. 3.5cm D. 14cm

**Celadon Incense Burner Qilin-shaped Lid**

—

Goryeo, 12~13C
Sea of Myeongnyangdaecheop-ro in Jindo
H. 10.8cm

297

**Celadon Incense Burner with Lotus,
Pond, Willows and Waterfowl Design**

—

Goryeo, 13C
Sea of Myeongnyangdaecheop-ro in Jindo
H. 15.9cm

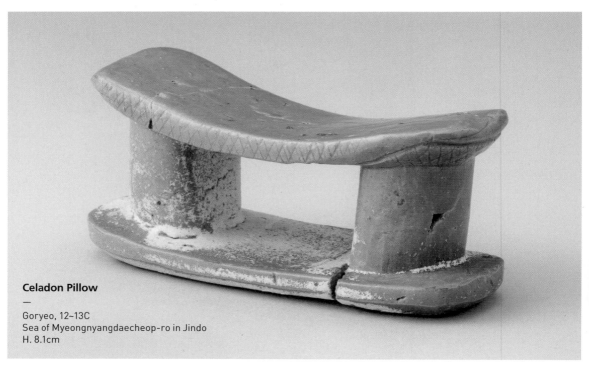

**Celadon Pillow**

—

Goryeo, 12~13C
Sea of Myeongnyangdaecheop-ro in Jindo
H. 8.1cm

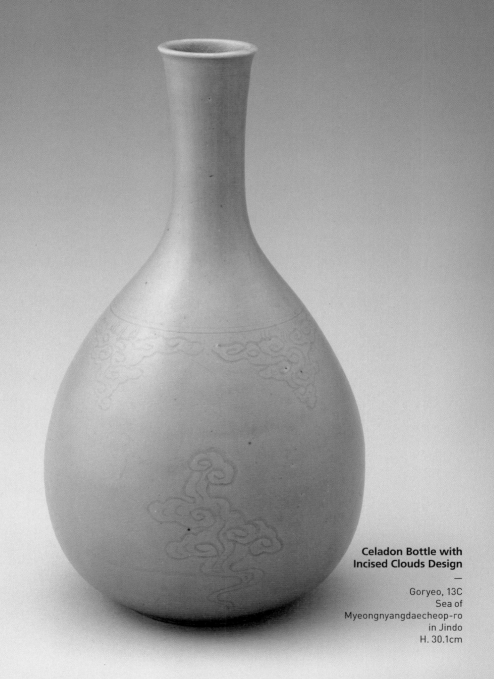

**Celadon Bottle with Incised Clouds Design**
—
Goryeo, 13C
Sea of
Myeongnyangdaecheop-ro
in Jindo
H. 30.1cm

**Celadon Dish with Inlaid Peony Chrysanthemums Design**

—

Goryeo, 13C
Sea of Myeongnyangdaecheop-ro in Jindo
H. 1.6cm D. 9.4cm

**Celadon Flower-shaped Dish with Incised Chrysanthemums Design**

—

Goryeo, 13C
Sea of Myeongnyangdaecheop-ro in Jindo
H. 2cm D. 9.5cm

**Celadon Flower-shaped Cupstand with
Inlaid Chrysanthemums Design**
—
Goryeo, 12C
Sea of Myeongnyangdaecheop-ro in Jindo
H. 5.6cm D. 9.6cm

**Celadon Jar with Inlaid Floral Scroll Design**
—

Goryeo, 14C
Sea of
Myeongnyangdaecheop-ro
in Jindo
H. 3.8cm D. 4.9cm

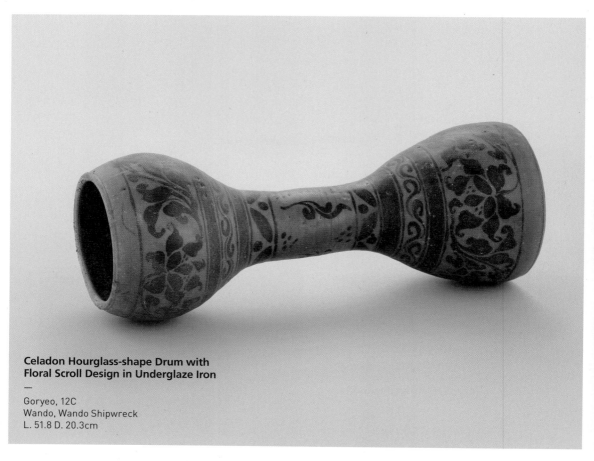

**Celadon Hourglass-shape Drum with Floral Scroll Design in Underglaze Iron**
—

Goryeo, 12C
Wando, Wando Shipwreck
L. 51.8 D. 20.3cm

**Celadon Prunus Vase
with Inlaid Willows and
Waterfowl Design**
—
Goryeo, 14C
Sea of Myeongnyangdaecheop-ro
in Jindo
H. 32.8cm

# Porcelain Vessels from the Shinan Shipwreck

**Celadon Kundka**

—

Yuan, 14C
Shinan, Shinan Shipwreck
H. 48cm

**Celadon Ribbed Jar**
—
Yuan, 14C
Shinan, Shinan Shipwreck
H. 23.8cm

**Celadon Incense Burner with
Lion Figurine on Lid**
—
Yuan, 14C
Shinan, Shinan Shipwreck
H. 16.5cm

**Celadon Long-necked Vase**

—

Yuan, 14C
Shinan, Shinan Shipwreck
H. 16cm

**Celadon Bottle with Two Handles and
Lotus and Floral Design**

—

Yuan, 14C
Shinan, Shinan Shipwreck
H. 19cm

**Celadon Vase with
Peony Scroll Design**
—
Yuan, 14C
Shinan, Shinan Shipwreck
H. 45cm

**Celadon Basin with Peony Design**
—
Yuan, 14C
Shinan, Shinan Shipwreck
H. 4.4cm  D. 19.1cm

**Celadon Figurine of
Woman**
—
Yuan, 14C
Shinan, Shinan Shipwreck
H. 19.7cm

**Celadon Bowl with Spout
and Spot Design**

—

Yuan, 14C
Shinan, Shinan Shipwreck
H. 5.4cm D. 16cm

**Celadon Melon-shaped Ewer**

—

Yuan, 14C
Shinan, Shinan Shipwreck
H. 6.4cm

**Celadon Lidded Case with Peony Design**
—
Yuan, 14C
Shinan, Shinan Shipwreck
H. 4.8cm D. 10.4cm

**Celadon Stem Bowl with Spot Design**
—
Yuan, 14C
Shinan, Shinan Shipwreck
H. 9cm

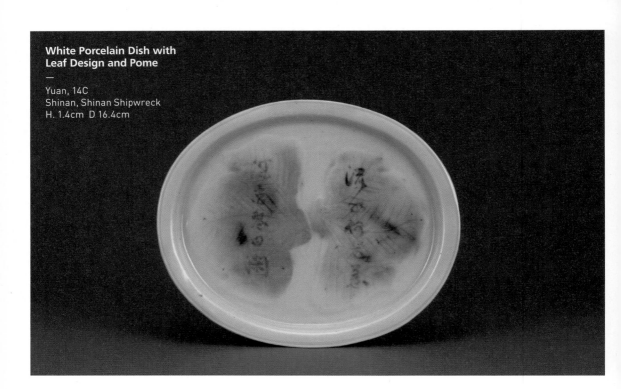

**White Porcelain Dish with
Leaf Design and Pome**

—

Yuan, 14C
Shinan, Shinan Shipwreck
H. 1.4cm  D 16.4cm

**White Porcelain Dish
with Parrot and Musk
Deer Design**

—

Yuan, 14C
Shinan, Shinan Shipwreck
H. 1.2cm  D 16.9cm

**White Porcelain Prunus Vase**
—
Yuan, 14C
Shinan, Shinan Shipwreck
H. 42.8cm

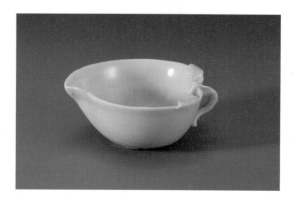

**White Porcelain Peach-shaped Cup**
—
Yuan, 14C
Shinan, Shinan Shipwreck
H. 3.5cm D. 7.6cm

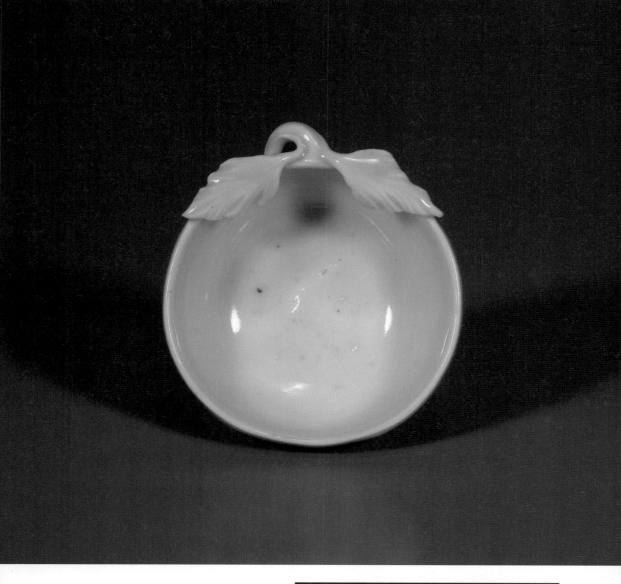

**White Porcelain Melon-shaped Cup**
—
Yuan, 14C
Shinan, Shinan Shipwreck
H. 2.3cm D. 6.7cm

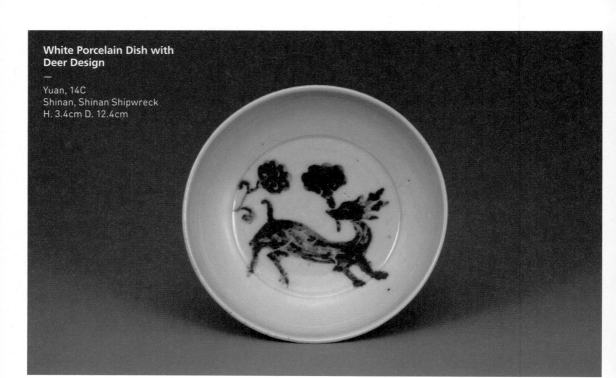

**White Porcelain Dish with Deer Design**

—

Yuan, 14C
Shinan, Shinan Shipwreck
H. 3.4cm D. 12.4cm

**White Porcelain Dish with Leaf Design**

—

Yuan, 14C
Shinan, Shinan Shipwreck
H. 1.6cm D. 15.1cm

**White Porcelain Three Taoist Immortals**

—

Yuan, 14C
Shinan, Shinan Shipwreck
H. 8.7cm

**White Porcelain Bottle with Two Handles**

—

Yuan, 14C
Shinan, Shinan Shipwreck
H. 17.3cm

**White Porcelain Bottle with Two Handles**

—

Yuan, 14C
Shinan, Shinan Shipwreck
H. 19.6cm

**Long-necked Bottle
with White Glaze
and Underglaze Black
Painted Wave and
Floral Design**
—
Yuan, 14C
Shinan, Shinan Shipwreck
H. 14.1cm

**Jar with White Glaze and Underglaze Black Painted Floral Design**
—
Yuan, 14C
Shinan, Shinan Shipwreck
H. 20.5cm

**Black Glazed Jar**
—
Yuan, 14C
Shinan, Shinan Shipwreck
H. 8cm

**Black Glaze Prunus Vase with
Peony Scroll Design**

—

Yuan, 14C
Shinan, Shinan Shipwreck
H. 27.8cm

**Black Glaze Prunus Vase with
Spot Design**

—

Yuan, 14C
Shinan, Shinan Shipwreck
H. 30.2cm

**Bronze Lion-shaped Incense Burner**
—
Yuan, 14C
Shinan, Shinan Shipwreck
H. 10.2cm

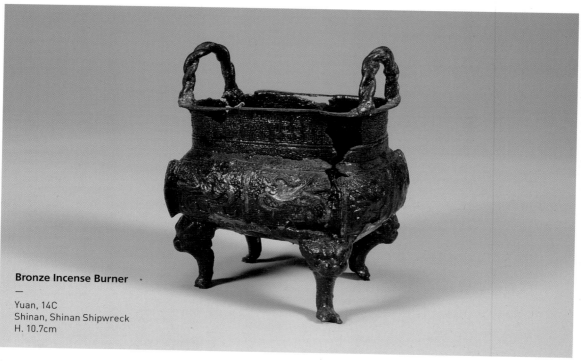

**Bronze Incense Burner**
—
Yuan, 14C
Shinan, Shinan Shipwreck
H. 10.7cm

**Brass Wine Goblet**
—
Yuan, 14C
Shinan, Shinan Shipwreck
H. 26.9cm

24p • National Research Institute of Cultural Heritage

25p • The Institute of Nautical Archaeology

28p • Incheon Metropolitan City Museum(2 photos)

29p • 〈Herald Corporation〉

40p • Crabster: Korea Research Institute of Shop & Ocean Enginering

56p • National Museum of Korea

57p • 〈The Kyunghyang Shinmun〉

59p • Cultural Heritage Administration, Cultural Heritage Administration(2 photos)

60p • Cultural Heritage Administration, Cultural Heritage Administration(4 photos, First and Second, Third, Fourth, Fifth)

61p • Cultural Heritage Administration, Cultural Heritage Administration(4 photos, Sixth, Eighth, Ninth, Tenth and Eleventh)

63p • Cultural Heritage Administration, Cultural Heritage Administration(2 photos)

61p • Celadon Bowl Inscribed with the Chinese Characters 〈使司帥府公用〉 (Shisishuaifgongyong): National Museum of Korea

66p • Coins, Wooden Tablets : National Museum of Korea

67p • National Museum of Korea

69p • National Museum of Korea(6 photos)

74p • National Museum of Korea

75p • National Museum of Korea(7 photos)

77p • National Museum of Korea(9 photos)

121p • National Library of Korea

125p • Two Artifacts from the Sinchang-ri Underwater Site: Jeju National Museum

125p • Celadon Bowl from the Sea of Jukdo Island in Boryeong: Cultural Heritage Administration

126p • Cultural Heritage Administration

131p • National Research Institute of Maritime Cultural Heritag · Gwangju National Museum

165p • Gimhae National Museum

166p • National Museum of Korea

167p • Photo, Gyeongju National Museum
• Plan, Cultural Heritage Administration

## • The Museum in the Book •

## Historical Sources

- 高麗史(*Goryeosa*)
- 高麗史節要(*Goryeosajeolyo*)
- 徐兢(*Xu Jing*), 宣和奉使高麗圖經(*Xuanhe Fengshi Gaoli Tujing*)
- 趙熙百(*Jo Hi-baek*), 乙亥漕行錄(*Eulhaejohaengrok*)
- 新增東國輿地勝覽(*Sinjeung donggukyeoji seungram*)

## Excavation Reports

- Cultural Properties Administration, 1981, *The undersea antiques, Shinan.*Ⅰ.
- _____, 1984, *The undersea antiques, Shinan.*Ⅱ.
- _____, 1985, *The undersea antiques, Shinan.*Ⅲ.
- _____, 1985, *The undersea antiques, Wando*.
- _____, 1988, *The undersea antiques, Shinan*.
- Gwangju National Museum, 2000, *Report on the Excavation of Heanam Sindeok-ri Celadon Kiln Sites*.
- Haegang Ceramics Museum, 2002, *Celadon Kiln Sites in Gangjin*.
- Mokpo Conservation Institute for Maritime Archaeological finds, 1993, *REPORT ON THE EXCAVATION OF JINDO LOGBOAT*.
- Mokpo National University Museum, 1992, *Green-Celadon Kiln Sites in Heanam Jinsan-ri*.
- _____, 2002, *Celadon Kiln Sites in Heanam*.
- National Maritime Museum, 1997, *The Korean Traditional Boat and Fishing Folklore*.
- _____, 1999, *The Korean Traditional Boat and Fishing Folklore Vol. 2*.
- _____, 1999, *REPORT ON THE EXCAVATION OF TALIDO SHIPWRECK*.
- _____, 2002, *The Korean Traditional Boat and Fishing Folklore Vol. 3*.
- _____, 2003, *The Underwater Remains of Doripo, Muan*.
- _____, 2004, *The Underwater Remains of Biando, Gunsan*.
- _____, 2004, *The Conservation and Restoration Report of Shinan Ship*.
- _____, 2005, *The Underwater Excavation of sea off Sibidongpado, Gunsan*.
- _____, 2006, *The Shinan Wreck*.
- _____, 2007, *Boryeong Wonsando Sea Site -submarine Excavation-*.
- _____, 2008, *Ansan Deabudo Sea Site -submarine Excavation-*.
- _____, 2008, *Gunsan Yamido Sea Site -submarine Excavation-*Ⅱ.

- National Maritime Museum and Shinan-gun, 2006, *The Excavation of Anjwaship, Shinan*.
- National Maritime Museum and Gunsa-si 2007, *Gusan Yamido Sea Site -submarine Excavation-*.
- National Museum of korea, 1996, *Report on the Excavation of kangjin-gun Yongun-ri Celadon kiln site-Plate*.
- _____, 1997, *Report on the Excavation of kangjin-gun Yongun-ri Celadon kiln site-Text*.
- National Research Institute of Maritime Cultural Heritage, 2009, *Taean treasure ship*.
- _____, 2010, *Taean Mado Shipwreck No.1*.
- _____, 2011, *Taean Mado Shipwreck No. 2*.
- _____, 2011, *Survey Report on the Waters of Mado*.
- _____, 2012, *The Conservation and Restoration Report of Dalido Ship*.
- _____, 2012, *Taean Mado Shipwreck No. 3*.
- _____, 2012, *Taean Wonan Beach Underwater Excavation*.
- _____, 2012, *Shipbuilding Technology of the Korean Traditional Ships IV: Jounseon(Tax Carrier)*.
- _____, 2013, *Chinese Ceramics Excavated from Waters off the Taean-Mado Area*.
- _____, 2014, *Incheon Ongjingun Yeongheungdo Shipwreck Underwater Excavation*.
- _____, 2015, *Waters off the Jindo Myeongnyangdaecheop-ro Underwater Excavation*.
- _____, 2015, *Shipbuilding Technology of the Korean Traditional Ships V: Mado Shipwreck No. 1, Taean*.
- National Research Institute of Maritime Cultural Heritage and Saemangeum Industrial Complex, 2009, *The Yami Island Underwater Excavation Ⅲ*.
- Wonkwang University Museum, 2001, *Report on the Excavation of Buan-gun Yucheon-ri Celadon kiln site-Plate*.

## Exhibition Books

- Gangjin Celadon Museum, 2007, *Special Exhibition of Celadon Excavated in Grave of Goryeo Dynasty*.
- Gyeonggi Ceramic Museum and National Research Institute of Maritime

Cultural Heritage, 2010, *Goryeo Celadons from the Sea*.
- National Maritime Museum, 2006, *Guide Book for Permanent Exhibits*.
- _____, 2006, *The Shinan Wreck and Ceramic Trades in East Asia*.
- _____, 2007, *The Metal Crafts in Shinan Wreck*.
- _____, 2008, *Goryeo Celadon Shipwreck*.
- _____, 2008, *Korean Ship and Shipbuilding Tools in the Modern Times*.
- National Museum of Korea, 2016, *DISCOVERIES FROM THE SHINAN SHIPWRECK*.
- National Research Institute of Maritime Cultural Heritage, 2009, *GORYEO CELADON SHIPWRECK AND GANGJIN*.
- _____, 2009, *Shipping of Tax*.
- _____, 2010, *Traditional Ship in the Paintings of Joseon Dynasty*.
- _____, 2010, *TIME CAPSULE OF 800 TEARS AGO*.
- _____, 2010, *DISCOVERY OF THE UNDERWATER CULTURAL HERITAGE*.
- _____, 2013, *Fragrant Vases Beautiful Maebyeong and Useful Jun*.
- _____, 2014, *Sea Routes in the South and West Seas of Korea Examining by Maritme Exchange Patterns*.
- _____. 2015, *MYEONG NYANG*.
- National Research Institute of Maritime Cultural Heritage and Incheon Metropolitan City Museum, 2015, *Gaosheng, a troop ship which was sunk during the War in 1894*.

## Books

- Kang, Kyung-Suk, 2012, *Korean Ceramics*, Seoul: Yekyong.
- Kim, Yoon Soo, Kim, Gyu Hyeok and Kim, Yeong Suk, 2004, *Wood Protection Science*, Daejeon: Chungnam National University Press.
- Kim, Byung Keun, 2004, *Study on the Trade Network in East Asia Based on the Materials Salvaged by Underwater Investigations*, Seoul: Kookhak jaryowon.
- Kim, Jae Geun, 1989, *History of the Korean Ship*, Seoul: Seoul National University Press.
- _____, 1994, *Korean Ship*, Seoul: Seoul National University Press.
- _____, 1996, *Korean Ship*, Seoul: Seoul National University Press.
- Suh, Dong-in and Kim, Byung Keun, 2014, *The Last Voyage of a Treasure Ship, the Shinan Ship*, Seoul: Juryuseong.

- Lee, Won Sik, 1990, *Korean Ships*, Seoul: Daewonsa.
- Choi, Wan-Gi, 2006, *Hanseon, the Traditional Korean Ship*, Seoul: Ewha Women University Press.
- Jeong, Ui-Do, 2014, *Study on the Ancient Korean Spoons*, Paju: Gyeonginmunhwasa.
- Kim, Yun-Jeong et al, 2015. *Dictionary of the Korean Porcelains*, Paju: Gyeonginmunhwasa.
- Chang, Nam-Won, 2007, *Study of mid Goryo celadons*, Seoul: Hyean.
- Kang, Kyung-Suk and Kim, Se-jin 2016, *Porcelain Vessels from Archaeological Sites*, Gwacheon: Zininzin.

## Journal Articles, Book Chapters, Proceedings, Theses and Dissertations

- Ahn, Gil-jung, 2006, *Study on marine transportation system of tax grains in the late 19th century : based on an officer's diary Johengilrok*, Unpublished Master Thesis at Sungkyunkwan University.
- Bae, Young-Dong, 1996, *Culinary Cultural Characteristics of the Korean Spoons and Chopsticks*, Munhwajae Vol. 29.
- Chang, Nam Won, 2001, *The Celadon of the 11-12th Centuries of Goryeo and the Popularization of the "kangjin Style,"* Arts History Association of korea.
- _____, 2004, *The Characteristics of Mid-Goryeo Celadons with Molded Design*, Arts History Association of korea.
- _____, 2008, *The Marine Transportation for Taxation, Ceramic Industry and Circulation in the Goryeo Dynasty*, The Association of Arts History.
- Choi Myeong-ji, 2009, *Study on Goryeo celadon excavated from the seabed of Daeseom, Taean*, Unpublished Master Thesis at Korea University.
- Han, Jeong Hoon, 2004, The Marine Transportation System(漕運制) and Sukdu Storehouse(石頭倉) of Masan(馬山) in the Goryeo Dynasty, *The Journal of Korean Medieval History Vol. 17.*
- _____, 2007, The Research of 13 Rice-warehouses and Traffic Route near Them in the Goryeo Dynasty, *The Journal of Korean Medieval History Vol. 23.*
- _____, 2009, Study of the tax transportation system in the period of Goryo Dynasty, Unpublished Ph.D dissertation at Busan National University.
- Han, Jung-Hwa, 2010, Chronicle and Production Site Presumed from Patterns of Articles Excavated off Wonsan Island, Boryeong, *Maritime Cultural Heritage Vol. 3.*

- Han, Sung-Uk, 2007, A Study on Goryo Celadons of intaglio 'O' pattern and '⊙' pattern, *Korean Antiquity Vol. 70*.
- Hong, Sun-Jae, 2009, A Study on the structure and type of Jindo-ship, Unpublished Master Disssertation at Mokpo National University.
- _____, 2011, Change in the Structure and Production Technology of Goryeo Shipwrecks, *Maritime Cultural Heritage Vol. 4*.
- Hong, Seung-Ki, 2000, Sasim(事審, Supervisors) and Hyangri(鄉吏, Functonaries) in early Koryo, *The Korean Historical Review Vol. 166*.
- Jang, Kyung-Hee, 2015, Bamboo Handicrafts of the Goryeo Dynasty through Underwater Excavation, *Maritime Cultural Heritage Vol. 8*.
- Joo, Kyeongmi, 2012, Cgaracteristics and Meanings of the Metal Objects Salvaged from Mado Shipwreck No. 3, *Taean Mado Shipwreck No. 3, National Research Institute of Maritime Cultural Heritage*.
- Ju, Young seon, 2010, A study on how old cargos were packed and loaded onto boats : With the focus on old Korean and Chinese ships salvaged from the sea, Unpublished Master Dissertation at Mokpo National University.
- Ko, Eunbyul, 2015, Research on Methodology for underwater zooarchaeological evidence, *Maritime Cultural Heritage Vol. 8*.
- Kim, Ae-gyung, 2008, Identify Characteristics and Production Periods of Celadon excavated off Wando, *Maritime Cultural Heritage Vol. 1*.
- Kim, Yun-jeong, 2009, Celadon Porcelain Cylinder with Lid Crafted in the 12th Century Goryeo: Its Distinctive Shape and Moldings, *Maritime Cultural Heritage Vol. 2*.
- Kim, Jea-Myoung, 2006, Tongyangchang(通陽倉) as a Section of the Marine Transportation System in Goryeo Period, *The Journa of Korean Medieval History Vol. 20*.
- Kim, Hyun-Jung, 2009, Bian Island Celadon Porcelains and Buan, *Maritime Cultural Heritage Vol. 2*.
- Lee, Jun-Gwang, 2010, Study on maritime transportation and excavated articles of Goryeo(高麗) celadon, Unpublished Master Thesis at Hong-Ik University.
- Lee, Jung-Shin, 2006, The Making Place of Copper(Dongso) and the Using of Copper in Koryo Dynasty, *Hanguksahakbo Vol. 25*.
- Lim, Kyoung-Hee, 2010, Classification of Wooden Tablets from Mado Shipwreck No. 1 and Their Meanings, *Taean Mado Shipwreck No. 1*, National Research Institute of Maritime Cultural Heritage.
- _____, 2011, Newly Deciphered Contents of Wooden Tablets:

Complementing Excavation Report *Maritime Cultural Heritage Vol. 4*.

• _____, 2011, Classification of Wooden Tablets from Mado Shipwreck No. 2 and Their Meanings, *Taean Mado Shipwreck No 2*, National Research Institute of Maritime Cultural Heritage.

• Mun, Gyung Ho, 2012, Study on the Tax Shipping System in Goryeo Period and Developing Instruction Materials. Unpublished Ph.D dissertation at Kongju National University.

• Nam, Tae-gwang. 2012, *Species Identification and Dating for the Woods Excavated from Jongmyo Square, Seoul, Korea*, Unpublished Master Thesis at Chungbuk National University.

• Park, Mi-Ook, 2006, *Study on the tomb furnishings in the Goryeo dynasty*, Unpublished Master Thesis at Pusan National University.

• Park, Ji-Young, 2008, The Research of Celladon Double-Headed Drum(Janggo) in Goryeo Period, *Maritime Cultural Heritage Vol. 1*.

• Park, Wonkyu, 2010, Tree-ring dating(dendrochronology), *CONSERVATION OF WOODEN OBJECTS*, National Research Institute of Cultural Heritage.

• Roh, Kyeong-jung, 2010, *Structural change research of Koryo Periodic ship*, Unpublished Master Thesis at Chonnam National University

• Shin, Eun-jae, 2012, The Character of the Grains Written in the Wooden Tags in the Wrecked Ships, Mado 1 and Mado 2, *History & Boundaries 84*, Pusan-Kyungnam Historical Society.

• Shin, Jong-Guk, 2012, Stonrware Jars Salvaged from the Goryeo Shipwrecks, *A Proceeding of the 36th Congress of the Korean Archaeological Society*.

• _____, 2012, Typology and Chronology of Stoneware Jars Uncovered in Goryo's Shipwreck, *Maritime Cultural Heritage Vol. 5*.

• _____, 2015, Study on the Utensils Used in Ships in the Goryeo Period. *A Proceeding of the Annual Conference of the Korean Medieval History Society*.

• Yoon, Yong-Hyuk, 2010, Anhungjong and Kaekgwans on the Western Sea Paths during the Koryo period, *History & Boundaries Vol. 74*.

• _____, 2013, Recent Research Trend on Goryeo Waterway and Island, *Journal of the Island Culture Vol. 42*.